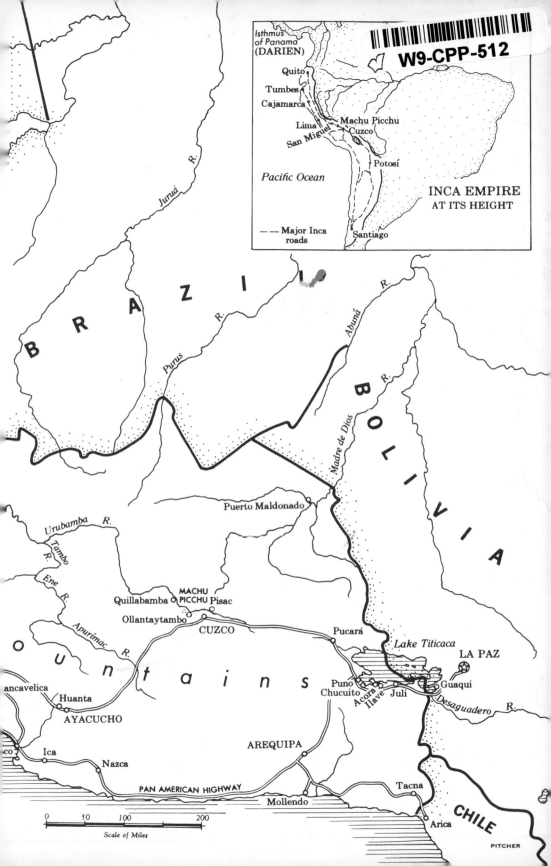

Isthmus
of Panama
(DARIEN)

W9-CPP-512

Quito

Tumbes

Cajamarca

Lima   Machu Picchu
              Cuzco
San Miguel

Potosí

Pacific Ocean

INCA EMPIRE
AT ITS HEIGHT

—— Major Inca
      roads

Santiago

B R A Z I L

Juruá R.

Purus R.

Abuná R.

R.

B
O
L
I
V
I
A

Madre de Dios

Puerto Maldonado

Urubamba R.

Tambo R.

Ene R.

Apurímac R.

Quillabamba   **MACHU
              PICCHU** Pisac
Ollantaytambo

CUZCO

Pucará

Lake Titicaca   **LA PAZ**

Puno   Guaqui
Chucuito   Acora Juli
           Ilave   *Desaguadero R.*

ancavelica Huanta
AYACUCHO

o   Ica
        Nazca

AREQUIPA

PAN AMERICAN HIGHWAY

Tacna

Mollendo

CHILE

Arica

0   50   100   200
       Scale of Miles

PITCHER

THE PERU TRAVELLER

THE
PERU
TRAVELLER
A Concise History and Guide

by SELDEN RODMAN

Ward Lock & Co. Limited · London

To

FERNANDO SZYSZLO AND BLANCA VARELA

without whose hospitality and friendship

Peru would have been more of an assignment

and less of a love affair

Made and printed by offset in Great Britain by
William Clowes and Sons, Limited, London and Beccles

ACKNOWLEDGMENTS

FOR the privilege of meeting and spending many hours talking with the two men whose vision is forcing modern Peru to reclaim its heritage—President Fernando Belaúnde Terry, and his political rival, Victor Raúl Haya de la Torre, the founder of APRA (Alianza Popular Revolucionaria Americana)—I am indebted to their associates and my friends Diputado Eduardo Orrego Villacorte and Diputado Andrés Townsend.

For their unique insights and sympathy with Peru's social problems, I am equally indebted to Emil Willimetz of Audio-Visual Productions, David A. Robinson of the American Studies Press, Tomás Loayza of the *Time* bureau in Lima, and John Davis, Director of the Art Center in Miraflores.

To John Davis, and to my friends to whom this book is dedicated, Fernando Szyszlo, the Peruvian painter, and his wife Blanca Varela, the poet, I am most indebted for opening the doors to Lima's cultural world and introducing me to such outstanding intellectuals as José María Arguedas, Emilio Adolfo Westphalen, Francisco Moncloa, and to the great collectors of Peruvian art, Pedro de Osma and Manuel Mujica Gallo, Alícia Bustamente and Reynaldo Luza.

Among my many friends at the American Embassy, at the time presided over by Ambassador J. Wesley Jones, the Counselor, Ernest Siracusa, and the Director of the United States Information Agency, Fred Barcroft, were most helpful. Also unfailingly kind and resourceful were Tom Crawford and Max Nicolini of USIA, Valentin E. Blacque, Consul, and Conrad Spahnholz of the Bi-National Center.

Two USIA men in the provinces, David Hakim in Arequipa and Hugo Huerta in Cuzco, made my visits to those cities unusually rewarding. Almost everywhere else in Peru it was the volunteers of the Peace Corps, directed nationally by Eugene Baird, who became my eyes and ears. Bob Manley, Gary Rohrs, Bob Marshall, Betsy Bess, Jerry Kling, Tom Heinz, Alice and Michael Dixon, David Frederick, Joshua Brand, David Copeland, Steve Most, Ellen Vaughn, and Barry Vogel were particularly helpful.

Traveling companions and friends in Lima or along the way who were fun to be with or shared their knowledge of Peru, or both, were: William Negron, Charles and Lucile Loeser in Trujillo; Arthur and Elizabeth Morris in Paita, Paul and Diana Goudey in Castrovirreyna; Maryknoll Father Anthony Macri at Juli; Glen H. Downs at Puno, Wilfred Lyons of the Santa Inez Mine; Jay and Edith Louthian, Marjorie Smith, Juan Francisco Gomez de la Torre, Gonzalo de Závola, and Nicole Hughes Maxwell (all at Iquitos); Carlos Parodi of Ayacucho; Carmen and Theodor Binder at Pucallpa; Russell Doonan at Tournavista; Caroline Crawford, James Wroughton, Bill Nyman, Robert Russell and the staff of the Summer Institute of Linguistics at Lake Yarinacocha; Haydée de Castagnola and J. Americo Olivares E. in Tacna; and in the capital Peter and Elizabeth Jones, Dr. Albert Giesecke, Augustín de la Puente, Erica Ruegg, Guillermo Revertér Pezét, Col. Carlos A. Rocca, Gala Smirnoff, Miguel Denegri Luna, Sam Donellon of ITT, and Donald Griffis, Sr., publisher of the *Peruvian Times*. Alfred M. Bingham, a son of Machu Picchu's discoverer and my former colleague on *Common Sense*, came to my aid with his memories, files, and photographs. Charles Duell, my constant friend and occasional publisher since 1940, believed in this book long before it was written and was the first to read it.

For their generous help with transportation facilities, without which this book could never have got off the ground, thanks go to Antonio Velarde, Director General of Aerolineas Peruanas, and his Miami representative, William Spohrer; to Antonio Bentín, Director General of Faucett Airlines, and his incomparably efficient and courteous representative in the Lima office, Jorge Sanjines Lenz; to Benjamino Rocca Muelle, Director of the Corporación de Turismo de Peru, and to his Sub-Director, Manuel Gutierrez, and to Carmen Gonzales Odriozola.

To Luis Vier, Director of Cooperación Popular, I owe a special debt of gratitude for lending me a truck and driver for the arduous trip through the Callejón de Huaylas, and for opening my eyes to the achievements of his organization's dedicated personnel throughout Peru.

PREFACE

As Guatemala to Middle America, or Italy to Europe, so Peru is the cultural seedbed to the huge continent stretching between Panama and the Antarctic. It is a continent incredibly rich and still largely undeveloped—and so is Peru, which holds the key to its coming of age. It always has. The promise has never been fulfilled; yet here, midway along the Andean spine, between the desert and the jungle, watering alike the Pacific and the Atlantic with its bounty, Peru from time immemorial has been a lodestar of wealth, the symbol of a possible unity without which all material treasure must be meaningless.

In pre-Columbian times, only the desert kingdoms of Peru gave visionary leadership. Their high arts in carved stone, gold, and ceramics were never equaled, and their engineering for collective welfare inspired the empire of the Incas to make of the whole continent an earthly paradise.

Whether the Incas' benevolent socialism, ordained by the Sun and controlled by the military, could have been extended beyond the borders of present-day Ecuador, Bolivia, and northern Chile, will never be known. The conquistadores of Spain, with Peru as their base, struck out over the whole land mass, and without developing the continent appreciably, they skimmed off enough of its movable wealth to enrich Europe, and themselves, for three centuries.

The great liberators, crossing the Andes from Argentina in the south and from Venezuela and Colombia in the north, inevitably converged on Peru and there fought the decisive battles against Spain. But the continent, and the world, were cheated again. Failing to unite, the noble visionaries sulked in their tents. Their armies merely usurped the places of the Spanish usurpers, perpetuating the monstrous exploitation of the land and the people. The provincial capitals of Lima and Quito, Caracas and Bogotá, La Paz and Santiago, Buenos Aires and Asunción and Montevideo became the capitals of separate states, warring on each other and tyrannizing their hinterlands.

Today, as before, Peru holds the key to the continent's oft-postponed fulfillment. Only Brazil has greater material resources, but Brazil is amorphous and without the tradition (or the common language) to take the leadership. Chile and Uruguay are better organized and more democratic, but they are predominantly "white" and wholly preoccupied with the struggle for self-sufficiency. The Argentine, dominated by an irresponsible military class, for better or worse faces Europe. Paraguay is a sterile dictatorship that has never recovered from the expulsion of the Jesuits. Venezuela and Colombia, with their great wealth in oil and coffee, are oriented toward North America, as least for the time being. Bolivia is too isolated, Ecuador and the Guianas are too small to involve themselves in the common destiny. But Peru, once again on the road to an indigenous solution of the Hispanic trauma, the continental dilemma, is eager to proselyte among its neighbors for a rebirth of Bolívar's vision of Pan America.

Deeper even than Mexico's are Peru's cultural roots. The empire of the Aztecs, unlike that of the Incas, with which it was contemporaneous, was mainly based on headhunting and military authority. The Incas *assimilated cultures*—without destroying either the monuments or the innovations. Their descendants, in adjacent Ecuador and Bolivia as well as in the Andean highlands of Peru itself, retain a measure of the pre-Hispanic culture to this day, waiting only to be convinced that the sovereign states are on their side at long last before sharing their heritage and carrying it into the industrialized lowlands.

The Mexican Revolution, to be sure, was far in advance of any similar movement to the south in giving social expression to the indigenous masses; but it made no attempt to speak for Latin America as a whole, and quickly hardened into a monolithic "institutional" party—nationalistic, paternalistic, capitalistic. The dominant social movements of contemporary Peru, on the other hand—Aprismo, Indigenismo, Mestisaje, Cooperación Popular—are Pan American in their philosophy and frankly intended by their leaders for export.

By the very facts of its peculiar, unique geography, Peru is equipped—as it always has been, potentially—to unite a continent whose tragedy has been its separatism. North to south, the country is divided into three regions as different as any on earth. The narrow Pacific coastal plain from Ecuador to Chile is desert. Broken very infrequently by a score of small, fertile river valleys, this desert might be thought worthless and inhospitable, but it is not. Here the great pre-Incaic cultures flourished. Here, where it never rains, Pizarro built Spain's capital, Lima—the cheerless but indomitable capital of Peru to this day. Here late in the nineteenth century, from the droppings of birds on the offshore rocks and from ni-trates in the sand itself, came fortunes in fertilizers. And today, from the millions of fish multiplying in the cold offshore current, come new fortunes in fish meal that have saved Peru from the in-flation ravaging its neighbors—an industry that might nurture a continent if put to wiser use.

Highland Peru, the sierra, rises close to 23,000 feet—in some places only fifty-nine miles from the Pacific, whose nearby Peru Trench is 26,000 feet deep! The Andes remain the sanctuary of the sons and daughters of the early civilizations to this day. It is hard for a lowlander to breathe and be warm in the windswept *puna* between the snowy peaks; but it is hard, too, not to be exalted breathing that rarefied air, and not to look disdainfully at mere national boundaries. Here a race of natural artists survives, sustained not so much by the daily sight of the blocky Inca fortresses and the only slightly less awesome string of Christian temples that stretches from Pomata to Cajamarca, as by concepts of craftsman-ship and beauty preserved in timeless isolation.

The third part of Peru (but far more than a third in size) lies like a sleeping giant. When roused, this is the part of the country that will drag the other two parts with it and join inevitably the slumbering vastnesses of the nations it adjoins. To try to fence the jungle would be as presumptuous and futile as to fence the ocean. The temperate, rain-drenched eastern slope of the Andes, the montaña, is ready to be colonized—it is fertile enough, they say, to feed all South America. The vaster climax forests stretching east are less immediately tractable; yet watered by the mighty Amazon and its tributaries, it is not inconceivable that they might feed the rest of the world. Yet . . . why should they? Has "civilization" any-thing comparable to offer in return? Here is to be found a rare, mysterious beauty: naked savages, intricately painted in rainbow hues, gorgeously arrayed with beaded diadems and feathers—the few thousand of them that have escaped the rubber predators and the missionaries. The setting itself has evaded the degradation of man—so far:

> The jaguar touches the leaves
> with his phosphorous absence,
> the puma speeds to his covert
> in the blaze of his hungers,
> his eyeballs, a jungle of alcohol,
> burn in his head.
> Badgers are raking the river beds,
> nuzzling the havens
> for their warm delectation,
> red-toothed for assault.
>
> And below, on the vastness of water,
> like a continent circled,
> drenched in the ritual mud,
> gigantic, the coiled anaconda.[1]

Curiously, there is no general book about Peru, in English or Spanish; nor is there any history from pre-Columbian times to the present. Treatises on the Incas and their predecessors abound in both languages, several of them first-rate and many of them in print. The major chronicles of the Conquest, and Prescott's incomparable history of it, are in paperback. There is a serviceable slim volume on the socio-economic development of Peru. There is a definitive study of the colonial architecture and sculpture. A few travel books, good, bad and indifferent, deal with Peru incidentally. The rest is silence. Why?

Peru is still outside the tourist's orbit. Most of those who fly to Lima—there is no other practicable way of getting to Peru—pass on to Santiago or Buenos Aires. No effort is made to hold them, and if they do diverge for three days or a week at most, an excursion to Cuzco and the nearby ruins of Machu Picchu is usually the extent of their curiosity. All-weather highways in Peru are confined to the desert littoral. The highland cities (including Cuzco), the villages famed for their folkcrafts and colorful festivals, the altiplano abounding in art which surrounds Lake Titicaca, and of course the jungles of the Amazon Basin can only be reached by flying over the Andes in local airlines, with unpressurized cabins. Oxygen must

[1] From *"Canto General"* in *Selected Poems of Pablo Neruda*, Edited and translated by Ben Belitt, published by Grove Press, Inc., copyright © 1961 by Grove Press, Inc.

be taken during all these flights—and even on the railway, the highest in the world, that plies laboriously between the capital and Huancayo. No hazard is involved, except perhaps to infants, but this is an experience the tourist has not yet "bought," and consequently the most exciting and varied panoramas and peoples in the Americas are denied him.

To permit him to read about what he is missing—and so perhaps make him resolve to go out of his way to see it—is not the only purpose of this book. Peru's history is a microcosm of three quarters of the world's. Under the millennial layers of its cultures it waits as ineluctably as China or India to be reborn in an incarnation the West least expects or wants. Stirring hopefully to the promptings of its continental destiny, it yearns to offer unity in the fragmented world of liberated colonies beyond the scope of primitive Africa or venerable Eurasia. To articulate these many Perus and open them to our obtuse perspective is this book's larger ambition.

CONTENTS

Preface   vii

Part I: HISTORY

Chapter 1. Pre-Columbian Peru: Despotisms for the
          Common Good   3
    Chavín de Huantar   4
    Nazca and Paracas   5
    The Tiahuanaco Invasion   7
    The Kingdom of Moche   8
    The Kingdom of Chimór, and Chan Chan   10
    Chancay   12
    The Inca Empire: Early Period   12
    The Inca Empire: Decline   15
    Welfare or Despotism?   16
    The Ruling Class   17
    The Commoners   18
    Crime and Punishment   20
    Paradise Lost?   21

Chapter 2. The Spanish Conquest: Despotism for Gold
          and Souls   22
    Preparations: The Three Voyages   23
    The March to Cajamarca   24
    The Capture of Atahualpa   26
    Ransom and Murder of the Inca   28
    The Founding of Lima   30
    Feuding; the Death of Almagro   31
    The Assassination of Pizarro   32

Gonzalo Pizarro Seizes Power   34
Pedro de la Gasca Restores Order   35

Chapter 3. THE COLONY AND THE LIBERATION   38
The "Black Legend"—True or False?   38
The First Viceroys Set the Stage   40
Social Classes under the Viceroyalty   41
The Sub-Empire of the Jesuits   44
From La Perricholi to Tupac Amaru II   46
Liberation's First Phase: Exiles' Return   48
José de San Martín in Peru   51
Simón Bolívar to the Rescue   53
San Martín and Bolívar Meet   55
From Guayaquíl to Ayacucho   56

Chapter 4. NINETEENTH CENTURY: THE WAR WITH CHILE   58
The Marshals of Ayacucho Seize the Spoils   59
Marshal Castilla Restores Order   61
Henry Meiggs and the Great Railroad Boom   64
Manuel Pardo Tries to Save Peru   67
Peru and the War of the Pacific: 1879–83   69
Aftermath: Cáceres and Piérola   72

Chapter 5. PERU TODAY: LEGUÍA, HAYA DE LA TORRE, ODRÍA,
BELAÚNDE   74
The Road to Despotism   75
The Dictatorship of Leguía   76
Haya de la Torre and APRA   79
Phase I: APRA Goes Underground   80
Phase II: APRA Veers to the Right   82
The Dictatorship of General Odría   84
The Presidency of Fernando Belaúnde Terry   87
The Program of Acción Popular   89
Under Fire from Right and Left   90
The Population Explosion   92

PART II: ILLUSTRATIONS   95

PART III: TRAVELOGUE

Tourists   131
Hotels and Communications   131
Lima and Its Environs   133

Beaches and Ruins   134
Churches, Museums, Collections   136
Trujillo and the North Coast   140
Cajamarca   144
The Callejón de Huaylas   146
Huancayo by Central Railway   149
Ayacucho and Holy Week   152
Cuzco   154
Machu Picchu, Ollantaytambo, Pisac   158
Puno and Lake Titicaca   163
Arequipa and Tacna   167
The Jungle I: Pucallpa   169
The Jungle II: Iquitos   173

Peruvian Chronology   182

Bibliography   184

Index   187

Part I
HISTORY

1

PRE-COLUMBIAN PERU: DESPOTISMS FOR THE COMMON GOOD

GLORY and mystery, even in times of recorded history, go hand in hand. We know a great deal about the ideal arts and exact sciences of Athens and Florence, but why they flourished amid the petty bickerings of these city-states that foundered in amoral violence has never been satisfactorily explained. There are socio-economic "explanations" for the unique political stability engendered by the North American Revolution of 1776, but attempts to account for the presence of so many farsighted statesmen to guide such a poor conglomeration of warring states are unconvincing. At least, in the case of the social and aesthetic glories of pre-Columbian Peru, historians are able to hide behind the absence of verifiable records. The Mayas and Aztecs farther north left dates and illustrated codices; in Peru nothing remains besides the artifacts themselves. No written language existed south of Guatemala, and what the Spaniards observed at first hand became distorted in the effort to justify their destruction of the civilizations they found. The mystery remains.

Part of the mystery is in the *site* of the early civilizations. It is hard to imagine a place or climate more inhospitable to man than the two-thousand-mile desert of Peru that runs along the Pacific from Ecuador into northern Chile. Rain rarely falls here because the moisture-laden winds crossing the Amazon Basin from east to west slam into the towering cordilleras, depositing all their burden on the *eastern* slopes. Only slightly less hospitable to man is the cold, windswept Andean plateau between the ranges. Yet in these

two unlikely regions the original migrants from the north settled—
and prospered.

Where did they come from? Overland from Asia, by way of the
Bering Strait, almost certainly. No trace of primitive or Paleolithic
man has ever been found in the Western Hemisphere. The Mon-
goloid strain is unmistakable in the Indian's coarse, straight black
hair, the epicanthic fold of the eye, and other traits. There is some
evidence, none of it conclusive, that there was contact between
these peoples and the Polynesians in the first millennium B.C. Easter
Island, only two thousand miles from Chile (to which it now be-
longs), was settled by Polynesians somewhat before the Conquest.
The return voyage to Asia, as Thor Heyerdahl in his *Kon-Tiki*
proved, is feasible in drifting rafts. The sweet potato, an American
root, was found in Polynesia by the earliest European explorers, and
was even known by its Peruvian name, *kumara*.[1] At any rate, the
Asiatic settlers of South America had established themselves for a
long time, perhaps for as long as ten thousand years, before the
first of the great cultures flowered.

Chavín de Huantar

Although hardy pioneers were already settled in some of the
twenty-four V-shaped river valleys that intermittently cut across
the leafless desert, it was not there, nor yet in the Andean valleys
the Incas came to favor, that the first great artists and planners
founded their citadel. Chavín de Huantar, unlike any other of the
pre-Columbian "capitals," lies east of the Continental Divide. Its
ceremonial center, southeast of the famous Callejón de Huaylas (*see*
pp. 146–148), was on a subtributary of the Amazon, but much too
high to be in jungle, a circumstance that led to the remarkable state
of preservation (until recently) of the so-called *castillo*, a three-story
structure with monumental sculptural ornaments, galleries, stair-
ways, and ventilating shafts. It was the study of this complex
structure by Julio C. Tello, thirty years ago, that led to the interest
in the Chavín culture and to acceptance of the theory that this was
the first of the "horizon" cultures influencing styles all over Peru.

Since the art of Chavín is primarily abstract, it tells us little of
the people who produced it. It is believed that the religious cult of
the Cat God, which its art celebrates, flourished between the years
850 and 300 B.C. Before this period there had been important utili-

[1] J. Alden Mason, *The Ancient Civilizations of Peru*. Baltimore, Maryland,
Penguin Books, Inc., 1957.

tarian advances. Crude pottery replaced gourds: the coastal valley Indians could now cook directly over fire. The llama and its cousin, the alpaca, the only large animals in the hemisphere susceptible to domestication, and native only to highland Peru, had become beasts of burden. Those uniquely New World plants, maize and the potato, began to rival fish and game as dietary staples. Garments made of pounded bark (as to this day among some jungle folk) began to give way to blue cotton cloth, some of it very crudely woven on a loom without a heddle. Early temples where llamas were sacrificed, built of stones laid in plaster, have been found in the Virú Valley. Here the native cameloid, the llama, was sacrificed in token of his already great service to man.

The leap forward to the nonutilitarian at Chavín is great. It has that quality of the miraculous that is invariably associated with revolutionary change. Just as the glass of Chartres, the frescoes of Giotto, the motets of Palestrina have a certain ultimate simplicity that could not be recaptured by later and greater artists, so there are many who claim for the austere, incised abstractions of the Chavín cult an aesthetic "rating" over anything produced by the cultures that were to follow. But in spite of the undeniably monumental conceptions and intricate linear decoration of these pioneer sculptors, their art has a coldness, an underlying cruelty that is forbidding to those who respond more to the human.

Nazca and Paracas

Humanism never develops without leisure, without time for reflection and preoccupation with the self. Another five hundred years would have to elapse before a truly organized society would be able to personify its achievements and foibles. This intervening period—roughly from 300 B.C. to 200 A.D.—effectively prepared the way. The semicivilized Indian communities were now firmly rooted in the coastal river valleys. Their greatest achievements were to be found in southern Peru, at Nazca and in the bone-dry caves of the Paracas Peninsula.

At least for the peoples of pre-Columbian Peru, the coastal desert had many advantages. Its rainlessness made it uninviting to the predatory tribes of highland and jungle; shelter was not washed away and clothing couldn't rot. (For similar reasons archaeology has prospered: the dry heat has been a perfect preservative, not only to bones and ceramics, but to ancient textiles.) The scattered river valleys provided part of the necessary food supply, and the ocean the rest. The cold 150-mile-wide Peru (Humboldt) Current, sweeping northward to Ecuador, not only lowers the equatorial land temperature but provides a unique supply of abundant marine life. Minute plankton nourish small fish of the anchovy and sardine variety. These in turn attract the larger fish—and clouds of pelicans and other sea birds. The birds deposit their droppings where they nest on the rocky offshore islands. This deposit, guano, is the most concentrated nitrogen fertilizer in the world. The only real hazard to life along the desert coast, apart from occasional earthquakes, has been the *Niño*, a warm countercurrent flowing south every seven years or so. Several times in a century Niño not only plays havoc with the fish-and-bird cycle but brings torrential rains against which the desert-dwellers (then as now) have no defense.

The cemeteries of Nazca, somewhat inland from the sea 250 miles south of Lima, were discovered by Max Uhle in 1901. The caves of Paracas, eleven miles south of Pisco in the same region, were first explored by Tello in 1925. Beyond the reach of the Niño, and undisclosed hitherto because of the absence of pyramids and other high structures, everything was remarkably preserved.

Nazca pottery—plates, slightly flared bowls, and jugs with a short stirrup-spout—are highly polished and then painted brilliantly against the brown or white backgrounds in shades of pink, buff, violet, black, and yellow. The subject matter—fish, birds, plants, and mythological combinations of all three—is handled with exuberance. Flat interlocking patterns are shaded and stippled. The treatment is stylized but not abstract, and because this art avoids scenes of daily life, it tells us very little of the lives of its makers. It is inferred that the Nazca people were peaceful and sedentary; they were ancestor worshipers but otherwise not religious. By far the most extraordinary of their accomplishments are the famous Nazca Lines, which had to wait for the airplane to be photographed—or even observed. Stretching across the tableland of the Palpa Valley, where rain has seldom fallen, these lines—some parallel, some intersecting, some in geometrical patterns, and some depicting mammals, birds, fish, and imaginary monsters—were formed by painstakingly removing the darker pebbles from the sand and piling them along the edges of the linear pattern. Since there is no elevation from which the figures may be seen, it is presumed that they were intended for the eyes of celestial beings. Miss Maria Reiche of Lima, a mathematician and astronomer who has spent years studying this phenomenon, believes that the straight lines, some miles long, served for calendrical observation; a series measuring 595 feet marks the summer solstice and the equinox. A carbon-14 test of a sighting stump at the end of one line established the date as 500 A.D., but many of the lines are believed to be older.

The mystery of the necropolis at Paracas is different. Who were the 429 old men whose mummies Dr. Tello found, buried with some of the finest embroidered mantles ever sewn? Not even the name of this culture has been determined; the Incas made no mention of it. Some of the great mantles found here were painted, but most were woven and then embroidered. As in ancient Greece, the colors were derived from insect and mollusk dyes. The textile arts became so very superior in Peru for two reasons: because the climate (cold desert nights) required warm clothing, and also because the highly developed agriculture provided the necessary leisure between harvesting and planting. Weaving requires a lot of time.

The Tiahuanaco Invasion

It was sometime during this intermediate period that the second of the "horizon" cultures swept over Peru. Its characteristics, in fact, were remarkably similar to those of Chavín. The invasion, if such it was, took place around 1000 A.D., and it almost surely originated in the celebrated Sun Gate of Tiahuanaco on the Bolivian side of Lake Titicaca. On that monolith are to be found the weeping face, the puma and condor heads, the trident and step design—all the alien elements that were to become familiar in the high arts of Moche, Chimór, and Cuzco during the next five hundred years. Even the megalithic stonework at the site, huge blocks fitted together with insets and tenons and copper clamps, prefigures the final horizon—that of the Inca Empire. No doubt it was the success of the Inca Empire's policy in deliberately obliterating the recorded (and remembered) history of its predecessors that has consigned the traces of this aggressive, wide-ranging religious cult to no more than the stylistic motifs it carried with it on its march.

Von Hagen speculates that the actual "invasion" of the coastal kingdoms by the Tiahuanaco "empire" began at Huari, hundreds of miles northwest of Lake Titicaca, where carved stones with crying eyes were found and whence an ancient road descends into the Pisco Valley.[2] This would account for the strong Tiahuanaco in-

[2] Victor Wolfgang von Hagen in *Realm of the Incas* (New York, New American Library of World Literature, Inc., 1957) and *The Desert Kingdoms of Peru* (Greenwich, Connecticut, New York Graphic Society Publishers, Ltd., 1965).

fluence in Nazca, spreading north beyond Lima to the Chancay Valley. From there the conquerors appear to have intruded into the outlying districts of the Mochica kingdom, already well established. For the Crying God abruptly appears in the ceramics of the Virú Valley, just south of modern Trujillo, flanked by the ruins of the Moche and Chimu capitals.

The Kingdom of Moche

The Mochica culture precedes the Tiahuanaco sweep, just as the culture of the kingdom of Chimór was to follow it. We know a great deal about these two because the Moches were thoughtful enough to "document" their way of life with the most realistic ceramics the world has ever seen, and the Chimus, though much less self-analytical in their art, were permitted to survive in Inca times and so became part of recorded history.

The Moche kingdom (or theocracy) is believed to have originated around the third or fourth century A.D. and to have lasted until its assimilation by Chimór around the year 1000. Judging by the immensity of its irrigation works and evidences of caste costume and specialization in pottery, it was an authoritarian state, highly organized and aggressive. Many of the engineering innovations once ascribed to the Incas originated in Moche. Mason calls the aqueduct at Ascope in the Chicama Valley "one of the great engineering triumphs of ancient Peru." Nearly a mile long and fifty feet high, it was built of 785,000 cubic meters of earth. The La Cumbre Canal, still in use, is even more astonishing. It conducts water in the same valley from a four-thousand-foot altitude to sea level. Its construction, dwarfing anything similar in Europe or Asia before Roman times, required, Von Hagen points out, careful planning: "The water could not flow too fast, or it would erode; if too slow, it gathered silt, in which plants rapidly grow; if neglected, it would cause rapid deterioration of the whole *acequia* system." By means of such ingenious works, by terracing, and by using guano for fertilizing their fields, the Mochicas extended the usable parts of the river valleys into areas that were once sterile sand.

In consequence, and no doubt employing unskilled labor and captured slaves quite ruthlessly, the ruling class had plenty of time to build monuments and perpetuate its own image. The so-called Temples of the Sun and the Moon, twin pyramids in the Valley of Moche a few miles south of the modern city of Trujillo, are built of millions of adobe bricks, and although they have lost their shape, thanks to the eroding wind, the torrential rains that beat upon them once or twice in a century, and the vandalism of treasure hunters, they are still impressive. The Huaca del Sol measures 750 by 450 feet at its base. The smaller Huaca de la Luna is surrounded by rooms with traces of frescoes on the walls. Arabesques in clay relief decorate other Moche sites in nearby valleys. Fortresses and thirty-three-feet-wide roads are also to be found.

Because the Mochica artist was a naturalist, we have a very good idea of what his people looked like, what they wore, where they lived, how they spent their time, how far their knowledge of the sciences extended, and even how they made love. Many of the ceramic jugs are portraits of actual people, handsome or ugly, "warts and all." Hook-nosed and high-cheekboned, Mochica man (women never appear except in a subsidiary role) painted his face, arms, and legs elaborately, wore a turban, ear and nose plugs, rings and other jewelry, and a colorful poncho over a breechclout. His teeth were excellent. Liquor, as with hard-drinking Peruvian Indians to this day, was *chicha*, boiled corn chewed and spit out to turn the starch enzymes into sugar, and then fermented. The home (*see* Plate 9) was well ventilated, with air ducts facing the ocean breezes, reminding one of Le Corbusier's "molded" structures. Bronze, gold, and silver were common, and were skillfully worked. Medicine and surgery were advanced, though it must have taken great faith or foolhardiness to be a doctor: the unsuccessful practitioner was sometimes buried alive with his victim. Herbs and curative powders were used, and thousands of trephined skulls that have been found all over Peru attest to the skill of surgeons who thus relieved pressure on the brain—presumably caused by blows from war clubs.

No other early civilization—or late one, for that matter—has left such an explicit record of its sexual life. Sodomy, fellatio, and other nonprocreative practices appear to have been common. There is no evidence that sodomy was indulged in between males, but its persistence among the Chimus seems to have troubled the Inca overlords because its practice in marriage in effect amounted to birth control, and like all aggressive empires, that of the Incas needed cannon fodder. It remains to be said that women and children are treated tenderly in the lifelike pottery of the Mochicas, and so are animals.

As everyone knows, there is more to art than being lifelike, and rarely does Moche's art transcend its fidelity to everyday life. It is an endearing art, but neither its forms nor its ideas are imaginative. One need not go so far as Sacheverell Sitwell, who finds the portrait vases "no better nor worse than Toby jugs, excepting that they are a thousand, or even fifteen hundred years old," but it is undeniable that the Mochicas were a self-satisfied, sometimes smug, people, with no desire to analyze or surpass their earthy materialism.

The Kingdom of Chimór, and Chan Chan

The art of the kingdom of Chimór, which absorbed the Mochicas about 1000 A.D. and was in turn absorbed by the all-Peruvian empire of the Incas some four centuries later, is of a greater dignity and aesthetic flair than that of Moche but tells us much less about its makers. The typical Chimu ceramic is "blackware," highly polished and elegant with a single spout at the center of its stirrup. At the three junctions of the pipe tiny figures, monkeys or birds, crouch —relieving the severity of the design but having no function or symbolic purpose. It is really in the arts of ornamental dress and precious metals that the Chimus excelled all Peruvians—all pre-Columbian Americans. One has only to visit the great Mujica Gallo gold collection in Lima (*see* pp. 137–139) to be convinced of this. Even the Incas were convinced: the Spanish conquerors found the craftsmen in precious metals in Cuzco to be Chimus all.

More than three quarters of all the gold objects found in Peru— and bear in mind that the Incas cornered the available supply in their time, losing it at one greedy gulp to the Europeans who turned masterpieces of art into negotiable bars—have been found in Chimu graves. As far back as 1550 an immense treasure in gold was revealed to the Spaniards near Trujillo by a local Indian who hoped that it would relieve the desperate poverty of his people. In 1566 another *huaca* near Trujillo yielded a million pesos in gold. A little later, gold seekers diverted an arm of the Moche River directly into the side of the Temple of the Moon; the temple collapsed and this time 800,000 ducats' worth was removed from the Mochica and Chimu graves. Two centuries later, Bishop Martínez de Compañon of Trujillo, encouraged by Charles III, put together a great collection of local pre-Columbian artifacts, including the first plan of the ruins of Chan Chan, the immense Chimu capital in the desert just outside Trujillo's walls, and shipped it to his appreciative monarch. The scientific curiosity of Charles III, the epoch-making voyage of Alexander von Humboldt under commission by Charles IV in 1802, the

later explorations and mappings of Chan Chan by the American
Ephraim Squier and the French savant Charles Weiner, prepared the
way for the assembling of the first great collection of pre-Columbian
art in Peru by Rafael Larco Herrera, a sugar *hacendado* of Trujillo
whose archaeologist son, Rafael Larco Hoyle, has classified according
to theme the sixty thousand pieces that have been called "the Rosetta
Stone of the Mochicas and the Chimu." [3]

The ruins of Chan Chan, covering six square miles outside the city
limits of Trujillo, are an unforgettable sight. This was much more
than a ceremonial center. It was a metropolis that may have contained a hundred thousand inhabitants. Aerial photographs have
revealed ten distinct tribal districts, and beyond the walls, as in our
modern cities, acres and acres of small family homes dribbling off
into the distance in planless disarray. Within the city proper the
streets were laid out at right angles to one another, flanked by houses
that had gabled roofs and gardens. Stone-lined reservoirs capable
of holding two million cubic gallons of water were fed by aqueducts
from the Moche River. It was when the Inca armies cut these aqueducts that the Chimu capital capitulated, and began to go to ruin.
The bases of the central pyramidal huaca and of the granaries that
surrounded it are still to be seen. The walls of molded adobe brick
are well preserved except where the infrequent cloudbursts, like the
disastrous one in 1925, have eroded their tops into a powder-white
rondure. In some cases the wooden lintels are still intact after a
thousand years of service. Yet there is something depressingly mass-
produced about Chan Chan. Chimu jewelry is never perfunctory;
but appliquéd plaster arabesques that appear to have once covered
all the major interior walls of Chan Chan—endless friezes of stylized
birds carrying fish, scorpions, crabs, etc.—have the look of having
been made with cookie molds, and indeed today's busy restorers
are replacing them for the tourists by just such a method without
any aesthetic loss except the blurring of time. The painting of the
walls, which may once have relieved this monotony, is of course
gone. It is the vastness of the gridiron itself, its vacancy, and the
thought of what it must once have been, peopled with throngs in
the vivid textiles and feathered robes and hammered breastplates,
that gives Chan Chan its *frisson* of romance.

[3] Von Hagen, in *The Desert Kingdoms of Peru*, has assembled the history of
Mochica-Chimu exploration in fascinating detail for the first time. *See* p. 137 of
the present book for a description of the Larco Herrera Collection, which has
now been moved from Chiclín in the Chicama Valley to Lima.

Chancay

One last pre-Incaic culture deserves to be mentioned. Perhaps because it does not fit into any large pattern, or perhaps because its locality is so close to Lima, the archaeologists have neglected it. But *as art,* the pottery, the free-standing "moon goddesses," and the painted textiles of Chancay have no superiors in the whole range of pre-Columbian Peru. The valley is thirty-five miles north of the capital. Its people were part of a subculture of the Chimu empire, a contiguous kingdom known as Cuismancu, which included such very large metropolitan sites as Cajamarquilla, a few miles up the Rímac River from Lima, and Pachacamac, a major tourist attraction (*see* p. 135) a few miles south of the capital. Only Chancay seems to have produced an original art style. The textiles, with their geometric designs applied in bold, slashing strokes, are highly prized by modern Peru's abstract artists. The black-on-white jugs, some of them very large, are covered with checkerboard designs in dots and lines that remind one of the visual illusionism of today's "optical" painting. Most spectacular are the moon goddesses. These pancake-flat figures, two to four feet in height, are pierced under the upraised arms and through the black crown, indicating that they were once suspended in the air. The almost neckless head with its enigmatic face is generally painted with a lateral black band passing over the protruding eyeballs—an effect of sunglasses. Parallel to this, above and below, an ornamental band of black filigree sets off the mouth and the hairline. Between the archaic stone carvers of Chavín de Huantar and the highland craftsmen of Huancayo and Ayacucho today, no Peruvian artists have handled form so inventively.

The Inca Empire: Early Period

No mean artists themselves, in domains as far apart as cyclopean stonework and painted wooden goblets, the people of the Inca Empire [4] are properly more renowned for their contributions to social engineering and statecraft.

[4] The term "Inca" as a designation for the people of this empire is inexact, but alternatives sometimes employed, such as "Quechua" and "Peruvian" are far more confusing. Originally the word "Inca" was applied only to the emperor-god himself, and to the group of related families in Cuzco whom the Spaniards called *"orejones"* (big ears) because of the heavy ear plugs their rank entitled them to wear. "Quechua" is now commonly used to refer to the spoken language of the Inca Empire, and to those of the highland peoples who still

Only a hundred years before the Conquest (1532), the Incas were no more than one of many highland tribes seeking to exert pressure beyond their particular valley. The valley of Cuzco is moderately broad and fertile, but it was exposed to raids from the wild jungle folk to the north and east as well as to the threat of the more powerful regimes along the coast. Partly to protect themselves from these threats, and partly perhaps because of innate capacities for organization and aggression, the Incas spent the first two centuries of their recorded history consolidating their position in the area immediately surrounding Cuzco and preparing the instruments for more ambitious extensions of power.

Legend sheathes the Incas' first two hundred years. Somewhere about the year 1200 A.D. Manco Capac founded the dynasty. From a place "with three windows"—sometimes identified with the caves of Tampu Tocco southeast of Cuzco [5]—Manco emerged with his brothers and sisters. As his direct descendants were to do, he made one of his sisters, Mama Occlo, his legal wife. He also got rid of his three brothers—thus preventing problems of succession that were to plague later Incas. With the sacred llama and a golden staff, he entered the valley of Cuzco, thrusting the staff into the rich loam to its hilt. Since this was obviously the place to settle, the aboriginal inhabitants had to be driven out—and they were. According to the sixteenth-century chronicler Garcilaso de la Vega, who was born in Cuzco and surnamed "Inca" for his royal descent, Manco and his sister were born on an island in Lake Titicaca, creations of the Sun. Garcilaso has Manco and the seven Incas who succeeded him conquering a good part of the empire, but other chroniclers and most modern historians have the extension of the empire beyond Cuzco and its environs begin with Pachacuti Inca Yupanqui (1438–71). Nevertheless it is accepted that Pachacuti's predecessor, the Emperor Viracocha, planned the expansion of the empire and established sway over the Quechua- and Aymara-speaking tribes between Cuzco and Lake Titicaca. One legend has it that Pachacuti seized the throne by force from the brother Viracocha had selected to be his legitimate successor—a bad omen.

---

speak it. (Aymaras, southwest of Cuzco and in modern Bolivia, speak Aymara.) "Peruvian" can only properly designate *all* the people of the modern state, regardless of whether they speak Spanish, Quechua, or Aymara. In this book the word "Inca" will refer to the emperor-god, and "the Incas" to his subjects.

[5] Hiram Bingham, Machu Picchu's discoverer, insisted that the locale should be identified with the Temple of Three Windows atop that fortress on the jungle's rim. *See* pp. 160–161.

The historical period begins with Pachacuti. In the ninety-four years that were to elapse before the Spanish Conquest, the Incas overran, pacified, and integrated an empire of 380,000 square miles —comprising all of modern Ecuador, Peru, Bolivia, and northern Chile, an area stretching 3,000 miles along the Pacific, equal in size to central Europe or to the Atlantic states of North America. Since almost all of this conquest was accomplished in the reigns of Pacha-cuti and his son Topa Inca (or Tupac) Yupanqui (1471–93), these kings have been compared with good reason to Philip of Macedon and his son Alexander the Great, for Philip conquered all the Greek states and his son extended the Hellenistic realm southward into Egypt and as far east as India.

Pachacuti began by sending his armies north under his brother Capac Yupanqui, conquering and impressing into service many tribes as he progressed. But Capac exceeded his orders, took Cajamarca, boasted of his accomplishments, and was executed. The Inca next turned south and east, completing the subjugation of the nations around Titicaca. To prevent rebellions he moved whole populations, replacing them with more reliable peasants who had been, as we say today, brainwashed. Under Topa, while still a prince, the empire's borders were pushed northward to Ecuador. The people of that re-gion were proud and cherished their independence, but "the cus-tomary conciliatory messages were sent to the chief of Quito, invit-ing him to join the pan-Andean co-prosperity sphere, which meant, of course, to yield to Inca arms and domination—or else." [6] The answer was No, and Quito was sacked.

Between Guayaquil and Chile there remained only the ancient kingdom of Chimór. The fortress of Paramonga and the great walls in the Chicama Valley had been intended by the Chimus to be their "Maginot Line" against barbarian invasion. But as in the case of the overcivilized French five centuries later, the defensive mentality proved no defense. Topa's armies simply outflanked these fixed posi-tions, and the King of Chimór was induced by his advisers to capitu-late gracefully. His sons were promptly sent to Cuzco to be "in-doctrinated with Inca ideology and to serve as hostages for their father's good behavior."

As emperor, Topa pushed eastward into Bolivia and southward as far as the Maule River in north-central Chile, where the fierce Araucanian Indians set the pattern for their heroic resistance to Spain later on. Topa in his last years seems to have succumbed to the

[6] J. Alden Mason, *op. cit.*

defensive mentality himself, for he built the mammoth fortress Sac-sahuamán on the bluff overlooking Cuzco—a formidable redoubt that gave the Pizarros as little trouble as Paramonga had given the young Topa.

The long, prosperous reign of Topa's son, Huayna Capac (1493–1525), saw the empire reach its maximum extent. It also saw planted the seeds of the dynastic quarrel that was to play into the hands of the conquistadores. At the time of Huayna's accession one of his half-brothers claimed the throne, and the claimant's mother was put to death for treason. Later a regent for the young king was executed for attempting to seize the power.

The Inca Empire: Decline

Huayna completed the conquest of Ecuador to its present Colombian frontier. But the empire was becoming too large for effective one-man rule from Cuzco. The Sun King, fearing treason and local uprisings—several of which he suppressed with the greatest difficulty—hesitated to delegate authority, and the problem of communication back and forth to Cuzco for even routine decisions became a monumental tangle. To be sure, the Inca system of highways and suspension bridges and messengers in relays was efficient, but even today the incredible terrain of Peru and its neighboring states defies quick transit by anything but the airplane—and not always by that. Rumors of trouble from without also plagued Huayna's last years. Indians from Paraguay who attacked the empire's outposts in Bolivia were accompanied by a white man, Aleixo Garcia, who had been shipwrecked on the Brazilian coast. It was also beginning to be known that white men in considerable numbers had established themselves in Panama and were making probing voyages down the Pacific coast of Colombia and Ecuador. A devastating plague, probably European smallpox or measles, was introduced from the north and ravaged the Inca lands.

It might have taken the Spaniards a century rather than a day, however, to topple the Inca Empire, had not Huayna Capac left the question of his successor in doubt. The legitimate heir, Huáscar, was duly installed in Cuzco. But Huayna's favorite son, Atahualpa, was supported by the army in Ecuador, where the dying Inca had spent his last years. Cieza de León compares the rival heirs thus: "Huáscar was clement and pious; Atahualpa ruthless and vengeful; both were generous, but Atahualpa was a man of greater determination. . . . He broke the law which the Incas had established, which was that only the eldest son of the Inca and his sister could be Lord-Inca, even though he had others who were older by other wives and concubines." [7]

Civil war ensued. A great battle took place at Riobamba between the rivals and their armies, and Atahualpa was the victor. The damage had been done. Atahualpa made his headquarters in Cajamarca to the north. The victory seems to have given him a sense of omnipotence bordering on infallibility. He destroyed all those who questioned his authority or counseled moderation. One Spanish chronicler claims that he personally cut off the head of a priest who prophesied that he would come to a violent end, but the credibility of this story is suspect as providing too neat a precedent justifying Pizarro's crime. Nevertheless Atahualpa did revenge himself savagely when Huáscar met final defeat at Cotabambas, near Cuzco, in 1532. The defeated generals and priests were executed. Their underlings were forced to pull out their eyelashes and eyebrows as offerings to the victor. Huáscar was obliged to watch as his entire family was slain and their heads raised on poles along the highway out of the capital.

But in Cajamarca, Atahualpa's hour of triumph was dampened by alarming news from the coast. The "white gods" had landed at Tumbes.

Welfare or Despotism?

It is in the nature of every revolutionary experiment for human welfare that its outcome is debatable. Consider the great French Revolution of 1789 and the Bolshevik Revolution of 1917. Were they steps forward in the human race's effort to free itself from degrading servitude? Or were they capitulations to naked terror resulting only in deeper bondage? A century and a half, and a half century, respectively, after the events, there is little agreement. And five centuries after the successful Inca bid to free the Andean peoples from economic insecurity, the question of whether this was accomplished at a price too high for human dignity is still hotly argued. It all depends, perhaps, on who answers the questions. Even under the murderous dictatorships of Robespierre and Bonaparte, the French bourgeoisie was "freer," economically speaking, than it had

[7] *The Incas of Pedro de Cieza de León,* edited by Victor Wolfgang von Hagen and translated by Harriet de Onís. Norman, Oklahoma, University of Oklahoma Press, 1959.

been under the monarchy. Similarly, the Russian proletariat and peasantry was better off under Communism than it had been under the czars. Only the intellectuals and professional classes are concerned about political freedom of choice.

The Indians of Peru have never been given a chance to opt for social welfare, or to escape from Western capitalism. But who can see them today and doubt that they were better off under the absolute authority of the Inca than they have been in the five centuries since Pizarro "freed" them? Only when disinterested intellectuals debate the question is the answer uncertain. To Louis Baudin, the French savant who reconstructs conditions as the chroniclers reported them, the subjects of the Sun God were provided for benevolently from birth to death, lived for the most part in peace and religious tolerance, and made of their labor a continuous fiesta.[8] But the dean of classical economists, Ludwig von Mises, introducing Baudin's book, warns the free world to be forewarned of a similar threatening fate. Pre-Columbian Peru, in his perspective, presents a terrifying "spectre of the human animal deprived of his essentially human quality, the power to choose and to act. These wards of the Inca were only in a zoological sense human beings. Actually they were kept like cattle in a pen."

How did the Inca system work? Whom did it benefit? Why did it so easily collapse? Is it revivable—or worth reviving?

The Ruling Class

As we have seen, the "socialism" of pre-Columbian Peru developed organically over centuries of time. It was the economic system of the pre-Incaic desert kingdoms, designed for man's salvation in a world of perpetual drought. The Incas only systematized it to give cohesion to their far-flung domain. There was no other choice. For on the high Andean plateau "everything," as Baudin puts it, "was inferior except man himself."

Baudin called the system of the Incas "a socialistic empire." Mason calls it "agrarian collectivism." "Theocratic communism" would describe it as well. The Inca was a despot but never a tyrant: since everything in the world by definition belonged to the Sun God, it was the Sun God's duty to see that his subjects produced as much as possible, shared equally in the common bounty, were cared for

[8] Louis Baudin, *A Socialist Empire: The Incas of Peru.* Princeton, New Jersey, Van Nostrand Company, Inc., 1961.

3

in childhood, old age, and infirmity, gave thanks through their happiness. Naturally, the welfare of the emperor and his household, the elite, and the army came first. But at least until conquest became an end in itself, there was more than enough to go around. Despotism was benevolent because, as Mason puts it, "the Peruvians had the proper idea that the higher the rank, the greater the required capability." Incest, as with the Egyptian Pharaohs, seems to have strengthened rather than weakened the royal strain.

As the empire grew, its ruling class expanded beyond the Inca's family. Officers of the army, the sons of conquered kings (kings were left in limited power so long as they swore allegiance to Cuzco), and finally administrators and technicians chosen for their ability were trained in the royal school—the *only* school. This school offered a four-year course: the Inca language, Inca religion, Inca history, the Inca accounting system.[9] Discipline was strict. Everyone from the Inca's sons on down was trained in obedience, courage, and physical endurance. The elite were exempt from taxation, which always took the form of labor, since there was no money.

There could be inequality in the *use* of land, but not in its accumulation, since land always belonged to the group rather than to any individual. Commoners contributed equally in their labor to the support of king, priesthood, and administrative elite—the only inequalities favoring those with many sons or many llamas. [10]

The Commoners

Since there was no "industry" in our sense—gold, silver, copper, and iron being extracted only to enhance the beauty of the royal court—agriculture and service in public works and soldiering were the only occupations of the masses of the people.

The basic social unit was the ayllu, a clan or kinship group made up of all the descendants of a common ancestor *except* the eldest son, who was cut loose at maturity to form his own ayllu. The ayllu

[9] Records, quotas, and accounts were kept throughout the empire by a device predating the Incas known as the quipu. A series of small knotted strings were attached to a larger cord, each string varying in color and texture, each knot in size and position. In accordance with the decimal system, census figures, agricultural stores in the provincial granaries (tambos), surplus equipment, available soldiers by age groups, disposition of llama herds, etc., could all be made into readily available statistics at the service of the emperor and his staff—in Cuzco, or on the march.

[10] This beast of burden was often received as an award for efficient service.

had the use of its own land, and was assessed for public service as a group. The collectively owned land was periodically redistributed by the state, to ensure rotation of crops and to lessen inequalities that might arise due to differences in the fertility of the particular plot; but private property in homes, orchards, herds, and personal possessions was permitted.

The ayllus were organized into village communities, or *marcas*. It was the business of the Sun God's administrator to assess these marcas in terms of their contributions and needs. After drawing up a relief map of the district and taking a census of the population and its collective wealth, the royal engineer would decide such matters as where terraces (*andenes*) should be constructed; how the available sources of water could be tapped, stored in reservoirs, and dispensed through canals; whether there was a sufficiency of fertilizers in the form of llama dung or guano (the Incas, knowing all about conservation, protected the offshore pelicans by royal edict, as well as the wild wool-producing vicuña and other valuable animals); how much seed would be needed to expand the plantings of maize or quinoa; whether markers were in place to denote the community's territorial boundaries; etc., etc.

What was produced was divided three ways. The division between the Sun (the religious establishment), the Inca (the central administration of the empire), and the district was not arbitrary. It depended upon the quality of the land. The community's basic needs must be met first. In hard times the people were fed and clothed from the surplus in the Inca's granaries. Baudin points out that although in the division of pasture land the share allotted to the Inca and the Sun was greater than that accruing to the community, much of this wealth actually came back to the commoners through the redistribution of accumulated stocks. Every head of a family received a pair of llamas, but the excess "constituted *a national reserve set aside for breeding,* to meet the needs of the entire population." A special set of fields, having priority even over those reserved for the Inca himself, was set aside for the incapacitated— widows, orphans, the blind, the ill, soldiers absent on military duty. No wonder that work on the Inca's share was regarded as an occasion for special jubilation and dancing in costume. "We can well understand," Baudin observes, "the astonishment of the Spaniards who were little accustomed to regarding work as a pleasure. Never has Fourier's dream of the 'attractions of labor' been more perfectly realized in this world."

Crime and Punishment

On the darker side, it cannot be denied that the commoners were given no voice in the making of the laws, or their enforcement. They may have enjoyed working and applauded their Sun God, but this rehearsed response was part of the regimentation of life from birth to death. The Incas understood well that leisure is the seedbed for dangerous thoughts, and on the few occasions when time hung heavy, new "works," no matter how unnecessary, were improvised. Sacsahuamán and Ollantaytambo may have been such boondoggles.

There were no prisons in Tahuantinsuyu, as the Incas called their kingdom, few thieves, and very little crime. Regimentation was too pervasive; society was too static. The threat of torture and death by clubbing was enough to give pause to acts of disloyalty or civil disobedience. These alone were unforgivable offenses. Theft and adultery were punished more severely when they occurred in the upper echelons than in the lower. There was no jury, and no appeal; trials were before state judges. In isolated cases of rebellion, the offending ayllu or marca was destroyed and its entire population put to death.

Cieza de León bears witness to the high morality of the Inca system. The people did not indulge in "eating human flesh, nor glory in their vices, nor were they headstrong or reckless, but, on the contrary, they corrected their faults. And if God had permitted that they have persons animated by Christian zeal, and not by greed, to teach them fully the precepts of our holy faith, they were people in whom it could easily have been inculcated." (This veiled rebuke to the hypocrisy of the Spanish missionaries is all the more noteworthy in view of the fact that the old chronicler was at pains to see his manuscript pass the censors of the Inquisition.) Further testimony to the honesty of the Indians under the Incas is given by the grandee who wrote to Philip II: "When they saw that we placed locks and keys on our doors they understood that it was from fear of thieves, and when they saw that we had thieves amongst us, they despised us." [11]

There was a good deal of drunkenness from the consumption of chicha, as there is to this day, but the physical and psychic relief induced by chewing coca was a privilege reserved strictly for the

[11] Quoted in *Lost City of the Incas* by Hiram Bingham. New York, Duell, Sloan & Pearce, 1948.

elite. It was only after the Conquest, when the Spaniards had everything to gain by keeping the Indians in a state of torpor, that chewing coca became the vice it still is in parts of the highlands. A puritan code in drinking, eating, sex, and manner of dress served the Incas well. Such a code was strictly enforced from the time of Pachacuti on.

Paradise Lost?

The strength of the Inca system was in its capacity to provide the Indian masses with sufficient food, clothing, order, and (within the limits noted above) elementary justice. This was an accomplishment that has not been achieved by any government in Peru since. The weakness of the system was in not providing sufficient freedom and initiative in the lower ranks. When the Inca was removed, his subjects were indifferent to changes at the top—at least until too late. What difference did it make who called the shots? But as the centuries passed, and the great terraces and irrigation works that sustained life fell into decay, and the Indians lost both their status and their land and were exploited mercilessly by the big *hacendados* and the small *patrones* alike, without receiving in return any of the security they had enjoyed in olden times, it began to be apparent that it *did* make a difference.

To revive the beneficent features of welfare socialism as practiced by the Incas is now the concern of every government in contemporary Peru that hopes to enlist the support of the Indian majority.

2

THE SPANISH CONQUEST: DESPOTISM FOR GOLD AND SOULS

THERE are many ways of looking at the Conquest, but the most surprising is the way it is accepted and even admired in Peru.

Outsiders in the West have reacted in three ways. "Realists" have accepted the justifications offered by the conquerors themselves: primitive "barbarism" must inevitably yield to "civilization"; Europe needed gold and overseas markets; the Church was obliged by the logic of its own doctrine to convert heathens to the faith. "Romantics" might deplore some of the means employed by Pizarro and his followers, but their admiration for the heroics of a band of 180 men who seized an empire and opened up a continent is primary. "Liberals," from Father Las Casas on down, have always characterized the Conquest as a base amalgam of piratical greed and religious hypocrisy foisted upon a defenseless race whose patrimony should be returned to them and whose institutions were in many ways superior.

This has been the position of Mexico since its 1910 revolution. There the comparatively beneficent Hernando Cortés is regarded as an unprincipled villain, and Cuauhtémoc, the leader of the Aztec resistance whom Cortés hanged, is the national hero. But in Peru, realists, romantics, and liberals alike are tolerant of Francisco Pizarro. His menacing, equestrian image in bronze flanks the Presidential Palace; and Mestisaje, a philosophical rapprochement of Incaic concepts of welfare planning with aggressive Hispanic individualism is the declared policy of Fernando Belaúnde Terry, the most Indian-oriented President Peru has had.

Preparations: The Three Voyages

Pizarro himself was certainly motivated by neither idealism nor religious evangelism when he set about gathering adventurers and financial backers in Panama for the first of three voyages along the western coast of South America. Promising to treat the natives fairly, and taking a priest or two along to convert them to the faith of Spain, was the routine procedure required to gain the Crown's sanction for every gold-seeking voyage that had followed Columbus. Columbus and those who followed him had already massacred or enslaved the entire peace-loving Indian population of the Caribbean islands. Cortés had destroyed the civilization of the Aztecs and subjugated the Mexicans. Alvarado had slain a million descendants of the Mayas and established the tyranny of Spain from Guatemala to Panama. Pizarro's path was beset with greater obstacles; but treasure was more than ever the sole objective, for rumors of a golden empire to the south had already filtered into Panama by 1511 when Balboa, the discoverer of the Pacific, had been shown trinkets of the precious metal and a drawing of a llama from the place the gold came from.

Pizarro had accompanied Balboa on the famous crossing of the isthmus. An illiterate swineherd from Trujillo in Estremadura, he had joined the gold rush when he first arrived on the island of Hispaniola in 1510. He was already forty when he met Cortés there, but though Cortés was a distant relative from the same Spanish province, he elected to join up with Balboa. Twelve years later, under Balboa's incompetent successor, Pedrarias Dávila, he found himself in Darien (Panama), the owner of an unhealthful tract of land and the usual *repartimiento* of sullen Indians. With Diego de Almagro, another soldier of fortune in his fifties, and Hernando de Luque, an ecclesiastic stand-in for a rich speculator, Pizarro began outfitting the first of three seagoing probes along the coast of Ecuador.

The first two were near-disasters. But Pizarro picked up enough tantalizing information about the Inca Empire to make him put up with wounds, disease, and empty-handedness. The legendary scene on the island of Gallo, in which the captain is supposed to have drawn a line in the sand with his sword and separated the men from the boys, took place. Tumbes, a port on the present frontier between Ecuador and Peru, was taken from its Inca garrison and converted into a base. Farther south, the site of modern Peru's third city,

Trujillo, hard by the ruins of Chan Chan, was considered worthy of the name of the captain's birthplace. A trip to Spain in 1528, where he was received by Charles V, confirmed Pizarro in the proceeds of his presumptive conquests—almost to the complete neglect of Almagro, who made the mistake of staying in Panama. A backlog of ill will between the partners, sufficient to destroy both of them and their families within a decade of the Conquest, was thus established.

The third voyage got under way early in January of 1531. Almagro remained in Panama as usual, to muster reinforcements. The company consisted of no more than 180 men and 27 horses.[1] Landing north of Tumbes, where earlier good relations with the Indians seem to have put the latter off guard, the Spaniards fell upon a town that contained a small treasure in gold and emeralds. Dividing this hoard among the company, after deducting the Crown's fifth, Pizarro sent back to Panama in one of his three small ships twenty thousand castellanos in gold. The presumption was that this would speed reinforcements, and it did. A hundred volunteers commanded by Hernando de Soto, later famous for his discovery of the Mississippi, arrived at the island of Puna in the Gulf of Guayaquíl just as the original band was recuperating from its first pitched battle with several thousand Indians. The fire power, tempered steel blades, armor, and cavalry of the Spaniards more than made up for the difference in numbers. Pizarro, from Cortés' experience, was well aware that this would be so; and when he now received intelligence of the civil war between Huáscar and Atahualpa, he remembered the brilliant use Cortés had made of dissension between Montezuma and his enemies.

The March to Cajamarca

At Tumbes, Pizarro now concluded that the time had come to change his image. How would the Indians react to good behavior? He gave orders that not a native was to be molested or robbed. Soon he was being welcomed with naïve hospitality, and even gifts of gold. "Everywhere," as Prescott says, "Pizarro made proclamation that he came in the name of the Holy Vicar of God and of the sovereign of Spain. . . . And as the simple people made no opposition to a formula of which they could not comprehend a syllable, they

---

[1] Garcilaso de la Vega puts the total still lower, at 160.

were admitted as good subjects of the Crown of Castile." [2] Of course the Spanish "colonists" in the rich Piura Valley had no intention of tilling their own fields, so a certain number of Indians had to be quietly enslaved, but as Francisco's cousin Pedro was to put it, "ecclesiastics and the leaders of the expedition all agreed that a repartimiento of the natives would serve the cause of religion, and tend greatly to their spiritual welfare, since they would thus have the opportunity of bing initiated in the true faith."

On September 24, 1532, Pizarro left the new colony with strict orders to treat the Indians in the surrounding countryside well lest his lines of communication be endangered. He had begun the historic march southeastward to Atahualpa's temporary capital, Cajamarca. Stripped down again to 180 men, the little band was confronted with the western rampart of the Andes. No sane military expert would have given Pizarro an outside chance of crossing over and successfully confronting the flower of a battle-hardened, never-defeated army of hundreds of thousands; yet of such daring strokes are the great military victories made. An attacker flouting the books, the mathematical probabilities, even common horse sense, is the contingency defensive hosts never reckon with.

Along the stages of the arduous ascent a battle of wits between Pizarro and Atahualpa now began. It will be recalled that the Inca had just won his throne by defeating his legitimate half-brother, Huáscar, and that the latter was being held in Cuzco pending Atahualpa's triumphal return to the Inca capital. Many of the conquistadores begged their commander to bypass the victorious army encamped at Cajamarca and march upon Cuzco. They reasoned that a "liberated" Huáscar, embittered by Atahualpa's cruel execution of his family and surrounded by still-loyal soldiers and functionaries, would have everything to gain by accepting the help of the Europeans in a campaign to regain power. But Pizarro had already sent envoys to Atahualpa, accepting the latter's gifts and offer of a generous reception in Cajamarca. Fully aware that a trap was being set for him, he argued that to turn south would indicate weakness and fear. Had he not already assured the Inca, in reply to the latter's boast of omnipotence, that great as were Atahualpa's victories and resources, they were as nothing compared to the powers of Charles V, whose legions were overrunning continents?

Upward and ever upward trudged the little band, from sub-

[2] William Hickling Prescott, *Conquest of Mexico and Conquest of Peru.* New York, Modern Library, 1936.

tropical gorges, through timbered forests, and finally into the icy, treeless wastes of the cordillera, where only the nimble-footed vicuña in the crags and the giant condor circling for carrion observed their struggles. Pizarro, as was his habit, performed the same chores of rock-lifting and bridge-building as his privates, participating in the same aspirations and jokes and curses. He was unique only in resourcefulness and single-minded insistence on victory. Incredible hardships and risks were undertaken at his insistence because, as Prescott notes, "he was not raised by rank and education above sympathy with the humblest of his followers."

Stone fortresses were passed, towering over defiles. The Indians had only to dislodge boulders, and the Spaniards below—who must have looked like ants—would have been crushed like ants; but the Indians watched them pass. On the seventh day of the ascent the oval valley of Cajamarca was revealed, "enamelled with all the beauties of cultivation," dotted with substantial homes, crisscrossed with irrigation canals. And along one ridge, dazzling the eyes of the presumptuous invaders, could be seen mile upon mile of war tents "as thick as snowflakes." On the fifteenth of November the weary Europeans entered Cajamarca.

The Capture of Atahualpa

What happened next is so fantastic that even eyewitnesses could not agree on the exact sequence of events. Pizarro opened negotiations by dispatching a squad of horsemen under De Soto to the emperor's headquarters. Atahualpa was wearing the imperial *borla* for the first time, and its fringe hung over his eyes. He listened without greetings or any expression while De Soto, without dismounting, informed him of the European facts of life and of Pizarro's desire to receive him. Hernando Pizarro, Francisco's elder brother, was informed that the Inca would visit their captain on the morrow. De Soto executed a flashy maneuver with his charger, reining it in on its knees directly in front of the emperor, who didn't flick an eyelash. Several attendants did draw back in terror, however, and they were reportedly executed that night. Some of the Spaniards thought that there was still time to withdraw with honor, but it was too late; the Incas would have annihilated them on the descent.

Pizarro now drew up his plan for the fateful meeting. The Spaniards had been assigned to stone buildings on the great square. Here the main body of soldiers would wait, and at a prearranged signal they would seize Atahualpa in the midst of his army! Had not Cortés seized Montezuma in Tenochtitlán? True, the Aztec monarch had acquiesced, and it had been accomplished without violence, but still . . .

Morning dawned on Saturday the sixteenth after a night full of apprehension. Cannon were placed, arms readied, and a solemn mass was performed in which Christ was invoked to judge the righteousness of "his" cause. "One might have supposed them a company of martyrs," Prescott says caustically, "about to lay down their lives in defense of their faith, instead of a licentious band of adventurers, meditating one of the most atrocious acts of perfidy on the record of history." At noon a great procession of Indians was seen approaching the causeway leading to the square, Atahualpa on a golden throne borne above their heads. But now what were the Indians doing? They were pitching tents! And soon the disquieting news came to Pizarro that the meeting would be delayed for a day. For the first time (and not for the last) Europeans were up against the maddening unconcern of Indians for keeping appointments. Pizarro knew that his men could never be keyed to this pitch twice. He sent back a message that everything had been prepared to welcome the monarch. And fortunately for the Spaniards, Atahualpa resumed his advance. Indeed he instructed his warriors to stack their weapons.

Preceded by sweepers and beaters, and accompanied by chants of victory ("which sounded in our ears like the songs of hell," one Spaniard recalled) the Inca in his collar of enormous emeralds entered the square, accompanied by six thousand of his bodyguards. Not a Spaniard was to be seen. When the procession stopped, the Dominican friar, Vicente de Valverde, came forward carrying a Bible and a crucifix and expounded at great length the doctrine of the Trinity. Garcilaso says the translation into Quechua was so bad that the phrase "One God in three persons" came out "God three in one make four." But the interpreter did make one thing clear: Atahualpa was to yield his supremacy to Pizarro in the name of some distant emperor and god. By whose authority? the Inca asked. Valverde pointed to the Bible. Atahualpa took it from him, threw it down (or dropped it accidentally) and exclaimed: "Tell your comrades that they shall give me an account of their doings in my land. I will not go from here till they have made me full satisfaction for all the wrongs they have committed."

Valverde picked up the Bible, rushed to Pizarro, and implored

him to give the signal. "I absolve you . . ." he shouted.[3] Promptly
a falconet was fired. In a cloud of gunpowder and trampling horses,
the Spaniards poured into the square and proceeded to massacre
their six thousand defenseless hosts. Within thirty minutes the holocaust was over. Atahualpa had been pulled from his throne and
securely bound. The *only wound* sustained by the Spaniards was
one that Pizarro himself received in his hand when he deflected a
javelin some panicky Castilian had intended for the Inca. Out of the
bloody square rushed the conquerors—but needlessly: the armed
host camped in the surrounding hills fled when they learned that
they were leaderless.

At this one stroke Pizarro was master of an empire stretching
from Colombia to central Chile, and had he been content to rule
through his stunned prisoner—or through Huáscar in Cuzco—the
history of Peru, and his own personal history, would have been
different. But acts of infamy have a way of generating their own
consequences; almost at once the guilty set about building defensive
snares into which they stumble.

Ransom and Murder of the Inca

Atahualpa, not without cruel deceptions of his own to weigh
upon him, was not sufficiently haunted by his treatment of Huáscar
to refrain, even in prison, from completing the ruin of his brother.
News that Pizarro contemplated bringing Huáscar before him to
judge which of the rivals deserved the throne inflamed Atahualpa's
jealousy. Upon his orders the gentle Huáscar was put to death, probably by drowning at Andamarca. By so doing, Atahualpa perhaps
hastened his own death. For pressure was now brought to bear upon
Pizarro to eliminate the man most likely to turn against him.

Atahualpa was not long in sensing that greed for the precious
metal the Indians called "Tears of the Sun" was the Spaniards' con-
suming passion. But though he succeeded in postponing his fate by
striking a bargain to fill a large chamber in Cajamarca with gold
in exchange for his freedom, he reckoned without his captors' duplic-
ity. The ransom chamber which exists to this day back of the great
square (*see* p. 144) was filled to the height of the Inca's upraised

[3] Garcilaso denies this generally accepted sequence. "How could one believe
or even imagine," he was to write, "that a Catholic father and theologian could
have said such a thing, at the most worthy of a Nero?" But Garcilaso, who
was not present, was also naïve enough to state that "Atahuallpa forbade his
men to fight through the intercession of Our Lord's mercy, who, on that day,
wanted to spare those who were going to practise His holy gospel."

hand with jewels, beakers, chains, and architectural decorations collected on his orders from all over the empire. Seven hundred gold plates were detached from the Temple of the Sun in Cuzco alone. The fact that many of the pieces were of priceless artistry meant nothing to the Spanish soldiers, who forced the Indian goldsmiths to melt them into uniform bars. The task of smelting consumed a month. The entire amount was found to weigh out in the value of 1,326,539 gold pesos. S. K. Lothrop in 1938 estimated its equivalent in dollars as $8,344,307. A like amount was melted down in Cuzco the following year, and half again as much was seized in Pachacamac and other places—twenty million dollars' worth all told, but many times that in purchasing power at the time.

With the ransom collected, the living Inca became a dangerous liability to his captors. De Soto and Hernando Pizarro are said to have grown fond of him. His jailors taught him to play dice and chess. But his own followers remained as much in awe of him as ever, and the messages constantly passing between them posed a threat of rebellion in the backlands. Almagro, who had finally arrived in Cajamarca with reinforcements, was especially insistent that the emperor must be disposed of. He was anxious to proceed to Cuzco and loot that treasure trove on his own. De Soto was sent to verify rumors of an imminent Atahualpa-inspired insurrection. In his absence the reluctant Pizarro was prevailed upon to bring the royal captive to trial.

The trumped-up charges were four. Atahualpa had usurped the throne and executed his brother. He was presently "squandering" Peru's resources. He was guilty of idolatry and adultery. He had tried to incite revolt. The Indian interpreter, who hated and feared Atahualpa, mistranslated the testimony of Indian witnesses. Not surprisingly, the Inca was found guilty. He was sentenced to be burned alive. "What have I done?" he asked Pizarro, "or my children, that I should meet such a fate? And from your hands, too, you who have met with friendship and kindness from my people, with whom I have shared my treasures, who have received nothing but benefits from my hands?" But the sentence was confirmed by Father Valverde.

The sun set on August 29, 1533, as usual. The man who believed himself to be its incarnation on earth was tied to the stake in the great square by torchlight. The Dominican friar approached him on the last of many unsuccessful missions to convert him to Christianity. The Inca was told that if he would consent to be baptized, he would die by the garrote instead of in the flames. Atahualpa agreed. The strangulation was performed. Pizarro and his cavaliers went into hypocritical mourning. And the following day De Soto returned with the news that the mutiny rumored to have been incited by Atahualpa did not exist. Pizarro, who had sent the Inca's powerful advocate away, and acquiesced in the captive's murder during his enforced absence, was wholly responsible for a crime that after five centuries still hangs darkly over Spanish Peru.

The Founding of Lima

How grimly appropriate that just five years later in Cuzco the man who had demanded most insistently that Atahualpa be executed was himself put to death by the Pizarros, and by the garrote. It would take the family of Diego de Almagro another three years to revenge itself on Francisco Pizarro, and another decade to help dispose of the entire Pizarro family, with which the Almagros had once been in partnership. The chaotic conditions and sporadic Indian uprisings resulting from this bitter family feud ensured that the Spanish viceroyalty of Peru would be governed with implacable severity in the three centuries to follow.

Pizarro's first step following the execution of Atahualpa was to find a puppet through whom the disintegrating empire of the Incas might be brought into some measure of control. The borla was duly placed upon the head of one of Atahualpa's willing brothers. Taking the young Toparca with him, the conquerors set forth upon the imperial highway from Cajamarca to Cuzco. At Jauja (due east of present-day Lima, in the Andes) a gathering host of Indians was scattered. But somewhere between that city and Cuzco, Toparca was killed, and though there was no evidence implicating the empire's most distinguished general, Challcuchima was burned at the stake. While the terrible Padre Valverde officiated, the Indian died protesting mildly that he "did not understand this religion of the white man." Pizarro was joined by another pretender to the empty throne, young Prince Manco; and accompanied by him, the Spaniards entered Cuzco on November 15, 1533.

Once more the loot was divided. One common soldier received as his share the huge circular gold plaque from the Temple of the Sun, and lost it the same night in a dice game. Indeed such an inflation of prices took place that a bottle of wine brought fifty gold pesos. Manco received the imperial borla from a new master of ceremonies—Pizarro. Valverde, newly installed as the first Bishop of Cuzco, officiated at the Coronation Mass. Don Pedro de Alvarado, Cortés' lieutenant and the conqueror of Guatemala, arrived to participate in the greater booty of Peru, but was bought off for a hundred thousand *pesos de oro*. He reembarked at Pachacamac, after being entertained there by Pizarro, and then the latter rode a few miles north along the Pacific beach to the banks of the Rímac River where, a little inland from the ocean, he laid out the streets of Peru's future capital. Since it was the day of the Feast of the Epiphany, he christened the site "The City of Kings," and Lima—as it came to be known from the sound of the river's Quechua name—has never quite forgiven the Conqueror for having selected a spot where it never rains and where for six months of the year the sun disappears behind a veil of dripping fog.

Feuding; the Death of Almagro

Pizarro's troubles now began in earnest. Almagro had been confirmed as Governor of the "southern" provinces, but two other Pizarro brothers, Juan and Gonzalo, were already there and not happy about yielding their suzerainty. The dispute was patched up momentarily, but meanwhile trouble was developing with the Inca elite in Cuzco. The sacrosanct "Virgins of the Sun" were debauched, and even Manco's wives were violated by the undisciplined Spaniards. Manco joined a general conspiracy, was arrested, and gained his freedom by promising to obtain for the greedy Hernando Pizarro a solid-gold statue of his father, Huayna Capac. Soon Cuzco was being besieged by an army of 200,000 disillusioned Indians. The stone buildings, all of which were roofed with thatch, were set afire. The great fortress of Sacsahuamán commanding the city was seized by the Indians. It was won back in a night assault by Juan Pizarro, who lost his life in the engagement. But the besiegers didn't withdraw. The entire country was now reported to be in arms. Four rescue parties were ambushed. Relief seemed to be only temporary when the entire besieging host was put on furlough to plant the fields. But Hernando and Gonzalo Pizarro conceived a bold stroke. The plan was to capture the Inca Manco in his headquarters, the great fortress of Ollantaytambo twenty-four miles north of Cuzco. The raid didn't accomplish its objective, but it served to disguise from the Indians the desperation of their oppressors. Manco retreated deeper into the mountains, perhaps to Machu Picchu.

Almagro, meanwhile, anxious to determine the value of his southern lands, had led a small army across the Atacama Desert of Chile as far as the frontier of the empire on the Maule River. In Arequipa, after the return journey across this fearful wasteland, the news of

Manco's uprising was brought to him, and he decided impulsively that the time had come to seize the rich Inca capital from the Pizarros. On the stormy night of April 8, 1537, his band entered the sleeping city, set fire to the Pizarros' headquarters, and bound the two brothers. Almagro was advised to behead them, but hesitated to go so far. Instead he proclaimed that Cuzco was his by "rightful" royal concession. When this news was communicated to Francisco Pizarro in Lima, the wily old conqueror persuaded his erstwhile partner to submit the whole dispute to "impartial" arbitration. Almagro was finally awarded temporary rule over Cuzco, but Hernando Pizarro was to be free and to leave the country.

No sooner was Hernando released, however, than he joined Francisco, who had been secretly assembling a large army. Hernando was put in charge of it, and on the twenty-sixth of April, 1538, Almagro's followers were defeated in a great battle. In July Almagro was tried for treason, sentenced, and strangled in the same Cuzco dungeon where he had held Hernando Pizarro. Once more the pious Pizarros went into mourning.

The Assassination of Pizarro

Gonzalo Pizarro was rewarded for his part in the murder of the venerable Almagro with dominion over those parts of Bolivia containing the mines of Potosí, soon to inundate Europe with silver. Hernando Pizarro, his ship loaded with gold, sailed for Spain, hoping to win royal sanction for the extension of the Pizarros' territory. But Almagro's friends beat him to Madrid, and instead he was clapped into jail, where he remained for twenty years, to emerge in 1560 humpbacked and babbling. The Spanish monarch was now sufficiently alarmed about the anarchy in Peru to dispatch a special envoy, Vaca de Castro, with powers to act as judge and protector of the natives, and to bring back a detailed report.

Francisco Pizarro, meanwhile, was seeking to lure Manco Inca into conference. Shuttling back and forth between Lima and Cuzco, he placed his younger brother Gonzalo in the governorship of Ecuador, and sent Pedro de Valdivia in the opposite direction to explore Chile. The embassy to Manco was not successful. The Inca received gifts and executed their bearer; whereupon Pizarro stripped one of the emperor's favorite wives, who had fallen into his hands, had her tied to a tree, beaten with rods, and then shot full of arrows.

Gonzalo Pizarro's brief reign in Quito was notable for the crazy expedition in search of cinnamon that led inadvertently to the discovery of the Amazon. After months of famine, crawling through the dense jungle and fighting headhunters as they progressed, the party finally reached the confluence of the Ucayali and the Marañón. Here they built a makeshift vessel, and Francisco de Orellano took off in search of provisions. For weeks Gonzalo Pizarro and the main body of Spaniards waited, eating reptiles and the leather from their saddles, until finally a wild-eyed white man appeared out of the eastern forests and told them what had happened. Orellano, arriving at the confluence of the Napo and the Amazon, had decided not to try to fight his way back against the current. He reasoned that it would make more sense to follow the big river to the Atlantic, sail for Spain, and claim the whole vast territory (Brazil) as his own. Gonzalo Pizarro's informant had protested the inhumanity of abandoning their comrades and had been put ashore to fend for himself. Orellano actually *did* get to Spain. And, even more remarkable, Gonzalo Pizarro and a remnant of his expedition made it back to Quito.[4]

Almagro's defeated followers waited for the King's envoy, hoping that he would side with them and rebuke the Pizarros, but when months passed and Vaca de Castro hadn't arrived, they decided to resort to violence. Diego de Almagro had had a son by an Indian woman of Panama, but though this son was present in Lima at the time, there is no evidence that he was taken into the plot to assassinate Francisco Pizarro. On the twenty-sixth of June, 1541, the Captain-General (and now Marquis) was having dinner in his palace with a company of his friends. The assassins stormed through the patio shouting war cries as if they were going into battle. The seventy-year-old Conqueror coolly gave orders for the door to be secured while he buckled on his armor, but the door was not bolted. Unarmored as he was, Pizarro slew several of his assailants, but the odds were too great. Soon he fell, and like Caesar received the blades of his killers. That night the young Almagro was paraded through the streets of Lima and proclaimed Governor and Captain-General.

No one denies Francisco Pizarro's courage, resourcefulness, and inspiring leadership, but no one denies either that he was driven by greed and ambition. By his inhuman treatment of Atahualpa and Manco he had alienated the Indians, and by his high-handed treat-

---

[4] Prescott's acceptance of Gonzalo Pizarro's account of his subordinate's "treachery" is disputed by later scholars who claim that Orellano never had a chance to backtrack on the swollen river. See *The Discovery of the Amazon, According to the Account of Friar Gaspar de Carvajal, and Other Documents.* Special Publication No. 17. New York, American Geographical Society, 1934.

ment of all the cavaliers except his relatives he had split the Spaniards into irreconcilable camps.

Gonzalo Pizarro Seizes Power

Vaca de Castro had now arrived in Peru. The scene was chaotic. Gonzola Pizarro was still in Ecuador. Young Almagro had fallen back on Cuzco and was preparing to avenge himself in the field upon his father's foes. The King's envoy, or "Governor," as Vaca de Castro called himself, had already shown signs of favoring the Pizarristas. Though still reluctant to side with Gonzalo Pizarro himself, he had alienated young Almagro by trying to win over his subordinates surreptitiously. On September 16, 1542, a battle took place between the two superbly armed adversaries at Chupas, near newly founded Ayacucho. In this battle more Spaniards were killed than had fallen so far in the entire conquest of Peru. Almagro was defeated. Fleeing to Cuzco, he was arrested by the magistrates he himself had appointed; and he was beheaded where his father had been strangled four years earlier.

The rule of Vaca de Castro was austere and did much to temper the exploitation of the Indians, but it was brief. The Dominican Padre Bartolomé de Las Casas had at last gained the ear of Charles V, and the emperor, horrified by Las Casas' account of what had been done to the Indians in his name and the name of Christ, decided belatedly to redress the balance. The "New Laws" of 1543 declared the Indians to be free. Those already enslaved might be retained for the lifetime of the enslaver only; but a clause specifically added that all Indians retained by those who had taken part in the "criminal" feud of the Pizarros and Almagros should be released. It was also ordered that Indians be moderately taxed, and be paid for their labor. To establish this code, which threatened to destroy the Pizarros and the other feudal lords of the Conquest, a viceroyalty was decreed for Peru, and a Viceroy, Blasco Núñez Vela, sent to enforce it.

Núñez' first act when he landed in Panama was to embargo a shipment of silver from the Peruvian mines—it had been extracted by Indian slave labor! His next act was to liberate three hundred Indians. The judges of the royal Audiencia in Panama were aghast. But much more horrified was the Spanish ruling class in Peru when Núñez landed at Tumbes and, to a proposal for compromise, replied frigidly: "I come not to discuss the merits of the New Laws but to execute them." Gonzalo Pizarro, whose brother Hernando was languishing in a Spanish jail, was least of all disposed to accept the authority of the new Viceroy. The moderate Indianism of Vaca de Castro had been about all he could stomach.

The colonists quickly rallied to Gonzalo's support. Only in Lima, where Vaca de Castro reluctantly protected him, was the new Viceroy well received. But even in Lima conspirators held secret meetings in support of Gonzalo. The hands of the heir of the Pizarros, moreover, were untied by the news that Manco Inca had been killed. It seems that a remnant of the Almagristas had taken refuge in his mountain fortress behind Cuzco, had quarreled with the resourceful young king during a game of chess, and had killed him. The visiting Almagristas in turn had been slain; but the murder had freed Cuzco from the recurring threat of another envelopment. However, the arrogant Viceroy sealed his own fate by imprisoning the one man who might have saved him, the moderate and loyal Vaca de Castro.

As Gonzalo Pizarro advanced on Lima with his army, Núñez retreated north along the coast to Trujillo. On October 28, 1544, Gonzalo entered the capital and was proclaimed Governor and Captain-General of Peru. The judges of the royal Audiencia administered the oath of office.

Pizarro wasted little time in pursuing Núñez up the coast. He caught up with him in Ecuador, and at Quito on January 18, 1546, the hapless Viceroy was killed and his army routed. Pizarro, following family custom, went into mourning. He was undisputed master of the former empire of the Incas.

Pedro de la Gasca Restores Order

As in all Renaissance tragedies, the last act in the drama of the Conquest left a good man in shaky command of the corpse-strewn stage. Just as the honest but colorless Macduff cleans up the wreckage of a kingdom left by the heroic Macbeth and his fellow rascals, so Pedro de la Gasca presided over the graveyards and empty treasuries of Peru after the last of the Pizarros had been driven from the scene.

By 1546 it was clear to Charles V that he had blundered. The New World colony that was enriching Spain beyond belief was in danger of being lost—if indeed it had not already been lost. Instead of confirming the wise and able Vaca de Castro in his powers, Spain had hurled upon her money-making colony a series of idealistic legal thunderbolts that would have been impossible to apply three hundred years later. On top of that, Madrid had dispatched to enforce this code a stupid martinet, Núñez, who had begun by alienating everybody in Peru and ended by getting himself killed and turning the last of the Pizarros into a virtually independent monarch. Only a man of unbelievable tact and ability would have any chance of reversing such a train of events, and by some miracle Charles V found just such a man. The Emperor was also astute enough to empower him with pardons for all who would come over to the royal side.

Pedro de la Gasca seemed the unlikeliest of instruments. He was an ecclesiastic, fifty years old, renowned mainly for scholarship, skill in theological debate, and judicious impartiality in settling questions of heresy. But he had demonstrated unswerving loyalty to the Crown and courage under attack. He accepted the mission with this unusual stipulation: "For myself I ask neither salary nor compensation of any kind. I covet no display or state of military array. With my stole and breviary I trust to do the work that is committed to me. Infirm as I am in body, the repose of my own home would have been more grateful to me than this dangerous mission. . . ." What La Gasca did demand, and receive, was authority over every civil, military, and judicial body in the colony; the right to grant amnesty as he saw fit; and revocation of the hateful New Laws. He was also furnished with an unlimited expense account and blank letters signed by the Emperor.

Arriving in Panama, La Gasca opened his campaign by sending conciliatory letters to Gonzalo Pizarro and the other rebels against royal authority. Next, with a subtle combination of diplomacy and bribery, he succeeded in winning to his side the commanders of the fleet on which Pizarro depended for communications and supply. Aboard this squadron of the turncoat Pedro de Hinojosa, La Gasca then sailed for Tumbes. Pizarro's allies in both the north and the south, sensing which way the wind was now blowing, began to defect to the royal envoy, taking the strongholds of Quito and Cuzco with them. Gonzalo's disciplined army shrank from a thousand to five hundred effectives. Once more La Gasca offered Pizarro grace. Once more it was rejected. La Gasca moved down the coast very deliberately, securing Cajamarca and Trujillo to protect his rear.

Pizarro won the first battle, at Huarina, with the help of his eighty-four-year-old chief of staff, Francisco de Carvajal, a pioneer in guerrilla tactics. This encouraged him to abandon the idea of either submitting, or retreating into Chile, where he might have held out for a long time. But Pedro de la Gasca, not discouraged at all, regrouped his forces and waited. He was joined by new allies:

Benalcázar, the conqueror of Quito, and Valdivia, who had opened up Chile. The Pizarro forces had retaken Cuzco, and La Gasca's first objective was to detach this city from the rebels. Carvajal was well aware that the royalist forces were throwing an Inca-type suspension bridge across the Apurímac, and he urged Gonzalo Pizarro to send him to this bottleneck for a lightning attack. Gonzalo preferred to keep the old man in Cuzco. He procrastinated, and finally sent an incompetent younger man. By so doing Pizarro lost his last chance. In a defensive posture, the rebels were no match for their foes. At Sacsahuana, near Cuzco, they were defeated—by desertion rather than arms. Pizarro's losses were fifteen men, La Gasca's only *one!* Carvajal was drawn and quartered. The flamboyant Gonzalo Pizarro was beheaded, and all his properties were turned over to the royal domain for redistribution.

Pedro de la Gasca completed his work in Peru within three years. He embarked for Spain in January of 1550. "The iron soldiery of the Conquest," as Prescott puts it, "required an iron hand to rule them." La Gasca's hand was not only of iron; within the context of distribution of the spoils and the creation of stability to ensure future efficient exploitation, it dealt fairly. The man was at once merciless and selfless. Even the Indians profited by the new order. The burden of taxation was reduced. Enforced shifts of population, an evil practice inherited from the Incas, was made illegal. The way was prepared for colonial Peru's Golden Age under the Mendozas and Toledo.

3

THE COLONY AND
THE LIBERATION

IN the 250 years between the reign of Viceroy Francisco de Toledo (1569–81) and the Battle of Ayacucho (1824), when the Spanish overlords were finally driven out, little of more than local significance transpired in Peru—or for that matter anywhere else in the vast colonial empire of Spain. The land and its people were given over to a systematic exploitation by the ruling classes of state and Church. Those Indians who survived became, in the words of the Peruvian historian García Calderón, "a nation of grown-up children."

The "Black Legend"—True or False?

Placing the blame for this state of affairs squarely upon the Spanish themselves came to be known in Spain as the "Black Legend," and in recent years most liberal historians have concurred. They take the position that the Spaniards were only doing what the British, French, and Dutch imperialists did (or would have done, given the same temptations). They argue further that the natives had enjoyed as little freedom and almost as much cruelty and poverty under their original ruling classes, and that the technological and humane achievements of Western civilization had to come and were worth waiting for.

The legend began, according to these revisionists, when Padre de las Casas overstated his case; if the conquerors had massacred the "millions" he claimed they massacred, there would have been no Indian survivors at all. Anglo-Saxon writers made a hero of Las

Casas, partly to further England's imperial interests at the expense of Spain's, partly to justify "benevolent" Protestantism vis-à-vis "demoniacal" Rome. Equally plausible is the case made by the revisionist historians for those Castilian kings from the emperor of Pizarro's time to Charles III at the end of the eighteenth century, who made a succession of good laws to curb the rapacious and protect the Indians; and for the hundreds of selfless priests from the compassionate early Franciscan and Dominican friars to the later Jesuits, who undeniably did much to alleviate the misery of their native flock.

Herring is at pains to point out that Spain "did not destroy ancient systems of noble moral standards: the Indians were masters of gluttony, drunkenness, sexual excesses, and refined torture," and he adds, "It is easy to overemphasize the pomp of kings and viceroys and to forget the much greater importance of the price of corn." [1] Baudin goes so far as to say that "the slave trade was no other than a humanitarian measure intended to relieve the natives of the most laborious tasks." [2] The splendid cities of the viceroys and the magnificently ornate churches erected by the Jesuits are cited as living proof of a "culture" without which the heathen would otherwise have languished.

But the case against the Black Legend crumbles when one turns from the exaggerations of its early advocates and the good intentions of an occasional king or prelate, to contemplate the actual condition of the masses under Spanish rule, the total lack of invention and originality in colonial culture, the disastrous vacuum of political institutions and standards for effective self-rule which became the heritage of the Spanish system as soon as the Spaniards had pulled out. Baudin, after doing his best to rehabilitate the viceroys (and forgetting the lyrical picture he has drawn of life and labor under the Incas) is finally forced to admit the evidence of his own eyes:

> The Indians are more backward now than at the time of the Spanish conquest.... They remain submissive, distrustful, and superstitious. *Intellectual torpor* constitutes their most marked characteristic and manifests itself in weakness of will, a taste for alcohol, unhygienic living, lack of proper nourishment as well as the most superficial knowledge of

[1] Hubert Herring, *A History of Latin America*. New York, Alfred A. Knopf, Inc., 1955.
[2] Louis Baudin, *A Socialist Empire: The Incas of Peru*. Princeton, New Jersey, D. Van Nostrand Company, Inc., 1961.

cooking, and an insufficiency of housing and clothing. Most of them continue to live in windowless huts of loose stones or mud, sleep with their clothes on, eat squatting on the ground.... Their very Christianity is only paganism disguised. Our civilization has passed over them as the wind passes over the Cordillera.... The Indian family has remained an economic institution, based on utility and sensuality, not upon sentiment. Dismal and dirty, it presents little that is attractive. Marriage is simply a mating arranged by parents and priest to initiate a life in common. Virginity in a woman, far from being valued, is looked upon with disfavor. As for the children, they must often do without the most elementary provisions of hygiene, and the infant mortality rate has become shockingly high.

The First Viceroys Set the Stage

It is generally agreed that the ablest of the viceroys were Antonio de Mendoza and Francisco de Toledo. Mendoza was the first of the two, coming to Lima from Mexico in 1550, the year Pedro de la Gasca returned to Spain. In Mexico, where he had served as viceroy for fifteen years, he established a great reputation for moderation and wisdom. He had kept the big landlords from unduly exploiting "their" Indians, had promoted modern methods of agriculture and stock breeding, and had encouraged the Dominican and Franciscan friars in their works of education and mercy. But unfortunately Mendoza died after only a year in office, and by the time Toledo arrived nineteen years later, conditions in Peru were almost as lawless as they had been under the Pizarros.

Francisco de Toledo was as ruthless as he was efficient, and his twelve-year span of office made it easy for all later viceroys to rule in order and indolence. When he arrived in Peru, several components of the colony's life had gotten completely out of hand. The enormous silver deposits of Potosí (now in Bolivia) were not yielding what the Crown expected. At the mines, and in a Lima already ringed with slums, workers were living like pigs. The clergy had joined the gold and silver rush and were paying little attention to the Indians. The latter, under Tupac Amaru, last of the direct Inca line, were harassing Cuzco from a hideout in the jungle-footed mountains.

Toledo solved the problem of the mines by modernizing methods of extraction. He also declared the rich mercury deposit discovered at Huancavelica a national monopoly. But his decrees guaranteeing the mine workers fair wages and working conditions "were almost universally evaded." [3] He reformed the clergy to the extent of insisting that the priests learn the native languages and remain in their parishes, but he increased the *cura's* power over the Indians through taxation (marriage and baptismal certificates, etc.), decreeing, for example, that an Indian marrying an "idolatrous woman" be given a hundred lashes. Dissident Indian communities were subjected to a Spanish version of the Incas' *mitimae*—they were shifted en masse to locations as distant as the swamps of Darien and the wastes of northern Chile. The mummies of the great Incas were removed to Lima lest their presence in Cuzco give courage to the Indians. And in the great square of the former imperial capital the captured Tupac Amaru was executed.

The implacable Proconsul returned to Spain, his job well done. There would be no further rebellions in Peru for two hundred years. Toledo had had massive fortresses built in all the principal cities. Ordinances were drafted to cover everything—there were seventy covering the cultivation and sale of coca alone. Within a decade the tribute paid to their *encomenderos* by 311,257 Indian serfs would amount to 1,434,420 ducats of gold annually. Yet Philip II, presiding over the military and naval ruin of the vast empire he had inherited, was not pleased with Toledo's success. At a chilling reception he is said to have remarked: "I didn't send you to Peru to kill kings but to serve them." The disillusioned nobleman is reputed to have died of a broken heart.

Social Classes under the Viceroyalty

In terms of its capacity to satisfy Spain's inexhaustible demand for mineral wealth and monopolized trade, the system that Toledo left behind him in Peru worked well. For a time it also worked well enough to keep the Viceroy and his underlings, the small landed aristocracy, and the Church rich beyond belief.

The Viceroy himself received a salary of thirty thousand ducats, and until late in colonial days was chosen by the king from the nobility. When Toledo's successor arrived from Spain, his wife was accompanied by "fifty damsels." With his authority extended to all

[3] Sir Clements Markham, *A History of Peru*. Chicago, 1892.

of South America except the Venezuelan coast, the Viceroy could afford such extravagances and still count upon retiring a very wealthy man. Toledo visited the provinces, but most of his successors preferred to luxuriate in the gardens of Lima, or behind the *miradores* (elaborately carved wooden balconies designed to protect the aristocracy from dust and the common gaze). They traveled from one social function to another in ornate carriages over paved streets; the idea of braving the roadless, bandit-infested mountains on horseback was unthinkable. In the remote districts the Viceroy's *corregidores*, and their deputies, the *alcaldes mayores*, became a law unto themselves. The corregidor was magistrate, tax collector, and policeman, and used all three functions of his office for personal enrichment:

> He could collect as he was able, pocket as much as he pleased, commandeer the services of Indians, and farm out their labor to contractors near or far. He could acquire the best land for himself and rob the Indians of their water rights at will. He could buy the Indians' wares at whatever price he chose to pay, and he could sell manufactured goods to them under threat of slavery or excommunication. We read of *corregidores* who forced their villagers to buy silk stockings, eyeglasses, and other preposterous items. The *corregidores* often used Indian chieftains as aides in their nefarious schemes, and many of these outdid the Spaniards in defrauding the simple Indians. Even more corrupt . . . were the *alcaldes mayores*, who were asigned to lesser communities and seldom received any salary.[4]

Under the Viceroy and the Audiencia (circuit court) through which he was supposed to rule, colonial society was rigidly stratified. All positions of importance went to the *peninsulares*, Spaniards from Spain. Next in importance, but not sharing in the top positions of army, Church, and state, came the *criollos*, Peruvian-born Spaniards. Since the only opportunity for the criollos lay in land, these became, as time went on, the hacendados, their *haciendas* becoming larger and larger through intermarriage or purchase—to make it possible for them to keep up with the peninsulares in the social whirl of Lima. Since the law required manufactured goods to be imported from Spain, prices skyrocketed; a handkerchief made out of a cent's worth

[4] Hubert Herring, *op. cit.*

of Peruvian cotton cost two dollars by the time it appeared in the Lima market. Lima was a lady's world:

> They are fond of white silk stockings, made extremely thin, that the leg may appear more shapely; the greatest part of which is exposed to view. These trifles often afford very sprightly sallies of wit in their animadversions on the dress of others. . . . Besides diamond rings, necklaces, girdles, and bracelets, all very curious both with regard to water and size, many ladies wear other jewels set in gold, or for singularity sake, in tumbago. Lastly, from their girdle before is suspended a large round jewel enriched with diamonds, much more superb than their bracelets, or other ornaments. A lady covered with the most expensive lace instead of linen, and glittering from head to foot with jewels, is supposed to be dress'd at the expense of not less than thirty or forty thousand crowns: a splendor still the more astonishing, as it is so very common.[5]

After the criollos in colonial society came the *mestizos* (mixed bloods)—mostly tradesmen, shopkeepers, and overseers. Then came the rudimentary "proletariat," cane cutters on the coastal sugar estates, laborers in those haciendas not worked exclusively by Indian serfs, domestics, and the like—the *castas*.[6] Finally came the Indians, still in the great majority, of course, and a much smaller number of imported Negro slaves.

It will be readily appreciated that the criollos were in the best position to rebel against the colonial system perfected by Toledo. It was they who finally broke the mercantile monopoly of Spain, setting up their own manufactories of wine, tobacco, chocolate, cereals, cotton, furniture, and metals; and it was they, when Napoleon occupied the homeland, who took over from the obsolete peninsulares.

[5] Jorge Juan y Santacilia and Antonio de Ulloa, *A voyage to South-America: describing at large the Spanish cities, towns, provinces, &c. on that extensive continent.* London, 1758.

[6] George Kubler in *The Indian Caste of Peru 1795–1940* (*see* Bibliography) points out that this term more fully conveys the status-bound character of these groups before and after the independence than such pseudobiological euphemisms as *mistos* (mixed bloods) or *cholos* (people with any percentage of white blood less than one half—a confusing term still in common use in Peru). It is significant that one cause of the criollo insurrection against Spain was outrage over the Royalists' belated attempt to free the Indians from the tribute they had always been forced to pay.

The Sub-Empire of the Jesuits

The role of the Church in colonial Peru is hard to assess fairly. It provided the only amelioration of the Indians' hard life, and it was responsible for almost everything worthwhile that has survived, from higher learning and agricultural science to architecture and the decorative arts; but by the same token it can be argued that without the veneer of charity and the costly, glittering facade of the churches the system would not have lasted as long as it did, and education would not have become the authoritarian practice that has stultified Peru's development ever since.

The early Dominican and Franciscan friars were mystics and crusaders who often defended the Indians, shielding them from the worst abuses and winning their hearts. It was their great achievement to identify the Christian God with Viracocha, the supreme creator deity of the Incas, and to merge such other Quechua symbols and institutions as the cross, the priesthood, the convents of virgins, and the belief in heaven and hell with their own. The ancient ritual dances and music were permitted in and around the new churches, a practice that continues to this day. The Inquisition, when it came to Peru in 1570, was a relatively benign phenomenon: it served to punish worldliness and heresy among the clergy, but the Indians were wisely exempted from the examinations and tortures reserved for the "higher breeds."

Very soon, however, the noble-minded friars were outnumbered by the secular clergy. These worldly ecclesiastics became embroiled with the civil authorities in a power struggle for the control of mines, land, and even slaves. Thornton Wilder, in a famous novel not unsympathetic to the Church, describes one member of the higher clergy thus:

> The Archbishop knew that most of the priests of Peru were scoundrels. It required all his delicate Epicurean education to prevent his doing something about it; he had to repeat over to himself his favorite notions: that the injustice and unhappiness in the world is a constant; that the theory of progress is a delusion; that the poor, never having known happiness, are insensible to misfortune. Like all the rich he could not bring himself to believe that the poor (look at their houses, look at their clothes) could really suffer. Like all the cultivated he believed that only the widely-read

could be said to *know* that they were unhappy. On one occasion, the iniquities in his see having been called to his notice, he almost did something about it.[7]

The record of priests who became oppressors and extortioners is grimly documented. The Peruvian historian Francisco Loayza tells of a priest who collected annually in fees: 200 sheep, 6,000 chickens, 4,000 guinea pigs, and 50,000 eggs, thereby increasing his salary of eight hundred pesos to as much as six thousand.

The militant Jesuits, who soon became the dominant religous order in the New World, were second to none as accumulators of all the secular goods and chattels, but with a difference. Their discipline and integrity never flagged. They labored in the vineyards. They never called upon even a slave to do work that they would not do themselves. They made no personal profit, nor did they practice extortion. Despite contrary examples on every side, they adhered to the code of sexual conduct for Catholic prelates. They fought the corregidores, and even the Viceroy himself, in defense of the 700,000 Indians who labored under their jurisdiction.

The empire-within-an-empire created by these thrifty, industrious priests was astonishing—and frightening to their slothful, corrupt rivals of Church and state. At the time of their ascendancy there were only two thousand Jesuits in all of South America, yet they built the most beautiful churches (*see* Travelogue), controlled almost all the nonmineral wealth of Peru, manufactured everything from bread and rope to leather and ships, virtually monopolized the fields of drugs and medicine, and were first in banking and external trade. It was they who built the schools, universities, and libraries and disseminated the ideas of the great scientists from Descartes to Newton. "Their success," Herring says, "was the reward of unfaltering consistency. Under their strict regime there was little time for recreation and none for sinning. Generation after generation they built up their power and accumulated their reserves." [8]

Inevitably the Jesuits ran afoul of the greater landlords, who seized upon their tax-exempt status as a means of terminating their "unfair" competition, and of the King, whose authority was flouted when they appealed over his head to God and the Holy Father in Rome. When in France the Jesuits went so far as to refuse absolution to the King's mistress, royalty made an unholy alliance with the ideological harbingers of the French Revolution who were demanding an

[7] Thornton Wilder, *The Bridge of San Luis Rey,* New York, 1927.
[8] Herring, *op. cit.*

end to ecclesiastical absolutism. Charles III came to power in Spain in 1759, and in 1767 this otherwise liberal monarch signed the edict ordering the expulsion of the Jesuits from the colonies. Their prosperous realm fell apart. The Indians despaired of salvation by peaceful means. The Church lost prestige from which it has never recovered. The colonial empire lost the only constructive element capable of holding it together.

From La Perricholi to Tupac Amaru II

The Viceroy who was in power when the Jesuits were expelled was an architect and military engineer by the name of Manuel de Amat y Junyent Planella Aymerich y Santa Pau. Appointed in 1761, he became something of a patron of the arts but gained more romantic fame through his mistress, a dancer named Micaela Villegas. It is said that the heroine-to-be of Offenbach's operetta gained her nickname from a habit the Viceroy had of shouting after her when she left him in a temper, "*Perra chola!*" (half-caste bitch). The legend, and a description of the charming pavilions Amat built for his mistress, would form a fittingly elegiac concluding chapter to the history of the viceroyalty of Peru, were it not that in 1780 the Indians made their last and most heroic effort to free themselves from the Spanish yoke. Amat had made a belated effort to quench the smoldering resentment of the criollos by conferring titles of nobility on Peruvians for the first time, but he would hardly have believed it if told that José Gabriel Condorcanqui, the young Marquis of Oropesa, would soon be leading an army of eighty thousand revolutionaries through the highlands of Peru, Bolivia, and northern Argentina.

The Marquis, educated by the Jesuits and confirmed in his considerable wealth by the Crown, preferred to be known by the name of his great Inca ancestor. He called himself Tupac Amaru II, and he began by exhausting every legal means to win redress for the virtual slaves of the highland mines, factories, and fields. In 1780, when the Viceroy and governors refused to discipline the rapacious landlords and corregidores, Tupac Amaru issued the call to revolt.

Indians responded in great numbers. The provocations had been increasing. In 1777, in violation of a law prohibiting their removal more than two miles from home, thirty thousand Indians from all over Peru had been driven to the mines at Huancavelica and Potosí; it was well known that most of them had died from the combination of altitude, fatigue, disease, fumes, undernourishment, rotting food, whippings, and torture. The so-called *yanaconas* (Indian personal servants) were treated little better. Corrupt customs officials took away from the sharecroppers what little the corregidores left. Herdsmen in the wilder provinces were being driven relentlessly toward the snow line. Royal orders sent to Viceroy Manuel Guiriór that might have eased the Indians' burden were simply ignored. Guiriór was recalled by Charles III, but the King's special envoy, José Antonio de Areche, raised the tax on the Indians by a million pesos!

Eight in lineal descent from Manco Inca (*see* pp. 30–35) and of the direct line of that Tupac Amaru who had defied Toledo, Tupac Amaru II was thirty-eight when the revolt broke out in 1780. He had taken command reluctantly, constantly affirming his allegiance to the Crown and the Church, and asking for nothing but an end of the abuses of the corrupt bureaucracy. He tried to enlist the support of the criollos and the clergy. The former feared reprisals from the military and perhaps sensed that the Indian masses, once in power, would demand much more than their moderate leader. Most of the priests, once Tupac Amaru had been excommunicated, rallied to the Spanish arms. Excommunication was also enough of a threat to keep many local Indian *caciques* out of action; and laws hastily announced by the panicky government in Lima abolishing repartimientos, tithes to the priests, and debts, had some effect. Yet the gentle Tupac Amaru swept all before him until on the heights above Cuzco he hesitated to press his advantage by seizing the city or burning it. On January 8, 1781, his poorly armed legions were hurled back by the royalist professionals. The desperate effort to free Peru had failed.

The terrible vengeance wreaked upon the Inca and his family, however, had two significant effects. It touched off a war of extermination between Indians and Spaniards from which the colony never recovered, and it ensured that the Crown would find no allies among the Indians when the criollos got around to launching their own independence movement fifty years later.

It was decreed that Tupac Amaru must witness the torture and executions of his wife, his sons, his other relatives, and his captains in the public plaza at Cuzco. Then his tongue was to be cut out, his body pulled apart by four horses, and finally his arms and legs set up on pikes in the four quarters of the rebellion. After the execution of this sentence, Areche engaged in a relentless manhunt for any other descendants of the Incas who might rally support among the Indians. He forbade the production of the ancient folk plays, the reading of Garcilaso de la Vega's *Royal Commentaries,* even the use of the Quechua language. There were, of course, the usual masses offered for the souls of the victims, and of course the customary wringing of hands over "colonial excesses" in Madrid, where the sensitive Charles III was reputed to have wept and even to have questioned the legitimacy of his title to the Indies. But though in the aftermath of the executions La Paz was besieged by another infuriated Indian horde, and the whole area around Lake Titicaca for a time joined the revolt, and eighty thousand more on both sides were slain, the Indian majority had lost its last chance to take a decisive part in the future of Peru.[9]

Liberation's First Phase: Exiles' Return

The liberation of Peru (and of all Spanish South America) from Spain is one of the great dramas in world history, comparable in its awesome setting and the recklessness of its heroes to the drama of the Conquest itself. And like the Conquest, but for different reasons, it was a tragic drama. Unlike the conquistadores, the liberators were idealists. They converged on Peru not for gold but to make men free. They took a kindly view of the Indians and their ancient ways of life. They were even concerned to unite the traditionally isolated states of the continent. But they were not prepared, either in temperament or by intellect, to take any of the constructive measures that might have achieved these objectives; and the dominant class in the states they entered was interested in nothing but dividing the Spanish spoils and continuing the *status quo* under its own tyranny. The noble liberators succeeded only in driving out Spain. Falling apart among themselves, many of them retired from the scenes of their triumphs to die in disillusioned obscurity. Only the memory of their heroism survives to inspire realization of the goals that eluded them.

Like all idealistic movements, the Liberation began in dusty garrets, dark libraries, clandestine conspiracies, and the eighteenth-century equivalent of the cocktail party—in the salons of those about to be overthrown. And as with most such movements, its progenitors were adventurers in exile, a motley collection of opportunists, cranks, and mystics.

The most famous of these was Francisco de Miranda. Miranda was a soldier of fortune whose only constant was a burning desire

[9] Lillian Estelle Fisher gives a remarkably documented account of these tragic events in *The Last Inca Revolt: 1780–1783*, published by the University of Oklahoma Press in 1966.

to see South America wrenched from Spain and placed under a native prince of the Inca line. Before he was forty-five, this young man of Caracas had met Washington, become the lover of Catherine the Great in St. Petersburg, intrigued among the Egyptians and Turks, and as a general under Doumouriez had been tried for high treason for "deserting" the French Revolution. When the Bourbons were decapitated in France, Miranda became the instigator of plots to overthrow their cousins in Spain. He made a fortune, lost it under Robespierre's dictatorship, finally turned up in London, where William Pitt the Younger gave him a small stipend to foment trouble against England's colonial rival. In the United States, Jefferson helped Miranda get a ship to liberate Venezuela—where he found that the Venezuelans had no wish to be liberated. When he returned there in 1810, Simón Bolívar, a rich young creole from Caracas, whom he had met in London, served under him as an officer. For a brief spell Miranda was appointed dictator of the newly liberated state. Then, in quick inexplicable succession in 1812, Bolívar lost the revolutionists' principal fort while making merry; Miranda, still with five thousand effectives, laid down his arms; and Bolívar, out of a combination of remorse and misguided patriotism, turned over his superior and old comrade to the Spanish. Miranda died in a Cádiz jail in 1816.

Another, and more fortunate, precursor of the liberation was Simón Rodríguez, Bolívar's tutor in the days before the latter was a jaded young millionaire in the capitals of Europe. Rodríguez, who had been to Europe and was an ardent disciple of Rousseau, taught the impressionable youth to hate the Bourbon kings whose agents had tortured Tupac Amaru. He also taught Bolívar to despise all clericals—except Padre de las Casas. Bolívar was instructed to identify himself, in his romantic search for glory, first with the wounded pride of his own class, the criollos, against whom the arrogant Spaniards discriminated socially as well as politically, and secondly with the downtrodden of all countries. Later, during Bolívar's years as a libertine abroad, it was Rodríguez who accompanied him from Vienna to Rome. He watched his pupil's ambivalent joy as Napoleon placed on his brows the iron crown of the Lombards, and he was present on the Aventine Hill in Rome when Bolívar swore, "In this city of Romulus and Sulla, of Augustus and Nero, of Brutus and Caesar . . . on my honor not to rest until I have liberated America from her tyrants!"

A dozen years later in Peru, when his brilliant pupil was as close to accomplishing that as he ever came, Rodríguez, who now called himself "Robinson," reappeared in South America. "I love that man like mad," said Bolívar with characteristic flamboyance. "Instead of a mistress I want to have a philosopher by me, for today I prefer the wisdom of Socrates to the beauty of Aspasia." (His Ecuadorean mistress, Manuela Sáenz, was in periodic eclipse.) So Rodríguez-Robinson was invited to journey south and climb Chimborazo with Rousseau's indefatigable disciple. Politely refusing this arduous assignment, he was appointed Inspector-General of Education and Social Welfare. In Bolivia he founded a model school, horrified the Catholic mothers by using his own naked body for anatomy demonstrations, and was charged by the amused General Sucre with squandering that new state's money on insane asylums as a means of "blotting out the Christian religion." But when Bolívar fell (Rodríguez was to survive him by twenty-four years), he refused to take any money, and when a fire destroyed his manuscripts in Quito, he declared: "That fire destroyed the chest which contained the happy future of the New World."

The third member of an improbable trio that gave the Liberation its contradictory ideological inspiration was not a man at all, but a legend. Lautaro, the name given by José de San Martín to the patriotic secret society he founded in Buenos Aires in 1812, was the idealized Araucanian hero of Ercilla y Zúñiga's famous epic of Chilean resistance to the Conquest. It was the legendary Lautaro who defeated Pedro de Valdivia in battle, and, reputedly saying to the Conquistador, "You came for gold, now we give you all you can use," killed him by pouring the molten metal down his throat.

Among the great libertarians of the time, Franklin, Miranda, Lafayette, Washington, were all high Masons. San Martín had met Francisco de Miranda abroad, and it is presumed that the Lautaro Lodge was organized on the model of the Carbonari and other masonic secret societies. In any event the people of the Viceroyalty of La Plata (which at that time included Bolivia) had become aroused by the capitulation of the Spanish Bourbons to Napoleon, and the thirty-six-year-old San Martín, who had won his military spurs in Spain, was ordered to prepare an army to march against the Spanish garrison in La Paz. San Martín had other ideas. He saw correctly that Lima, capital of the Viceroyalty of Peru, was the real stronghold of Spanish power in South America. With little or no help from Buenos Aires, he carefully prepared a small army of five thousand men, crossed the Andes from Argentina into Chile, defeated the Spaniards in the two great battles of Chacabuco and Maipú, inducted his young Chilean ally, Bernardo O'Higgins, into the Lautaro Lodge, and leaving liberated Chile in his charge, took ship with his victorious army for southern Peru.

José de San Martín in Peru

He was the noblest of soldiers—so selfless and morally upright that he could not but fail in the dirty game of politics. But for a brief period it was his happy lot to be permitted to act as a soldier-statesman alone. Whether or not his rigorous character was his by birth, it certainly was tempered on the Napoleonic battlefields, and by an incident in Madrid, where duty to the moribund royal cause stood in the way of his coming to the aid of a friend who was being lynched by a mob. He became taciturn, speaking only when spoken to, repressing his love for the arts, never dancing, remaining faithful to his wife in the Argentine through all his campaigns, taking no pleasure in honors or decorations or titles—Bolívar's exact opposite except in genius and courage.

Short of the Andes when the government in Buenos Aires fell, he was urged to return and make himself dictator, but the idea of killing fellow countrymen for personal power repelled him, and he continued on to Chile—in the face of false accusations that Chile was bribing him. Receiving a huge purse there in gratitude for his victories, he turned it over to the founding of a public library with the words, "Education is the master key that opens the door to prosperity and makes a happy nation."

Landing at Pisco, San Martín advanced against the Peruvian royalist forces with such careful preparation and such successful efforts to make enemy regiments defect that in the victory at Cerro de Pasco there were only fifty-eight dead. He could have taken Lima by storm, but preferred to wait. The hard-line Viceroy, Pezuela, was finally forced to give way to the liberal General La Serna. Then San Martín met with La Serna and calmly pointed out that, though the latter *might* win, "How long can a few hold out against the millions who demand freedom?" The Spaniards were reportedly touched, and they were amazed when San Martín continued: "Let there be appointed a regency, designated by the viceroy, which would rule an independent Peru until an agreement is reached in Spain about a prince of the reigning house who would take the throne of the new nation." The Viceroy agreed in principle. There was a banquet at which San Martín proposed a toast: "To the fraternity of Europeans and Americans!" But of course the royalist army rejected the great Liberator's moderation, and indeed the times were anything but prepared for it. San Martín has been maligned as a royalist at heart, but he himself stated his position quite clearly: "My whole desire is that this country should be ruled by itself, and *only* by itself. As to the manner in which it governs itself, that does not concern me in the least." [10]

San Martín moved toward the capital of Peru, still cautiously. Indians, and Negroes from the river valleys, flocked to his standard. His agents in Lima won recruits to freedom. Lord Cochrane's fleet, which had transported his army from Chile, blockaded the capital's port, Callao; but with Lima starving, San Martín saw to it that food passed through his lines. "The soldiers are my enemies only on the battlefield." On July 9, 1821, Lima capitulated. And on the twenty-eighth San Martín proclaimed the independence of Peru.

The anomaly of this puritan in voluptuous Lima is nowhere more poignantly brought out than in the anecdote of the friar who visited him the day of the entry and compared him to Caesar and Lucullus. "Good heavens!" said the dour general to his aide after the friar's exit, "What are we going to do? This is not promising." Everything that could be done to seduce the Protector of Peru, as he now called himself, was done. He was embraced by swooning women at gala receptions. He was taken to balls (one wonders what he thought of the *tapadas*, women veiled to show one eye, or of those who smoked their cigars in the orchestra) and to bullfights. Aristocrats, like the Marquis of Torre Tagle, joined his cause, doubtless to protect their vast estates. His friendship with Rosa Campusano was compared by society to that between Amat and La Perricholi—much to San Martín's discomfort. But the Protector proceeded quietly with his reforms while Lord Cochrane fumed at the failure to attack the royalists in Callao or in their mountain stronghold at Jauja.

He abolished the Inquisition. He established freedom of the press. He opened the country to free trade—and almost immediately Callao gave up without a shot being fired. He recognized Peru's public debts, including the royalist ones. He established a library, as he had in Santiago. He created a Peruvian Legion under the English General Miller and the Frenchman Brandsen. He even appealed to Spaniards to return and enjoy the new freedom. Distinctions of race and class meant nothing to San Martín.

It could not last. The freebooter Admiral Cochrane absconded

[10] Ricardo Rojas, *San Martín, Knight of the Andes*. Translated by Herschel Brickell and Carlos Videla. New York, Doubleday & Company, Inc., 1945.

with 586,000 pesos belonging to the people—he was later to defect from Chile too, serving her enemy Brazil. Torre Tagle defected to Spain. The Spaniards now began to receive reinforcements from the sea. Their army greatly outnumbered Peru's and was better equipped. And it was at this precarious juncture that San Martín received word that Bolívar, fresh from his triumph in liberating Colombia and joining it to Venezuela, had crossed the Andes in the north and was approaching Quito, the capital of Ecuador. Bolívar addressed flattering letters to San Martín in Lima, offering even to serve under him, but his arbitrary action in seizing Ecuador without any plebiscite and annexing it to Greater Colombia filled San Martín with forebodings. Nevertheless he sent aid to Bolívar's lieutenant, José Antonio de Sucre, already marching into northern Peru, and he himself took ship for Guayaquíl for the fateful meeting with his great contemporary.

Simón Bolívar to the Rescue

One sometimes wonders what would have happened had Peru come up with a liberator of her own in 1821–22. Perhaps there would have been no room for him. General Miller, Marshal Sucre, Lord Cochrane, the Protector San Martín—their motives were relatively easy to understand and their actions predictable; but the character of Simón Bolívar is so altogether irrational as to defy analysis. It is agreed that he was thoroughly "Spanish": devastatingly magnetic to women, and that he pursued as an end in itself "glory" rather than mere power (certainly not profit). But there the agreement ends. Was he really interested in freedom for others? Was he a dictator or a democrat? Honest or full of guile? Humane or ruthless? Ahead of his time, or behind it? The answers are inconclusive.[11]

The early years of Simón Bolívar—in Caracas, in Europe, and back in Caracas—were not conducive to developing a sense of responsibility. At the gaming tables and the glittering all-night parties of Napoleonic Europe, nothing seems to have disturbed the young millionaire criollo except the sense of his social inferiority to the Spanish grandees and a nagging desire to emulate Napoleon's imperial triumphs on the one stage still empty and accessible to him. Bolívar matured only in the course of acquiring power, and in many respects he remained a delayed adolescent until he had lost everything he sought. That, of course, is part of the fascination of Bolívar's

[11] See Salvador de Madariaga, *Bolívar*. New York, Pellegrini & Cudahy, 1952.

personality. Warmth, gaiety, inspirational eloquence, and impulsive generosity he never lost.

Nor can he be blamed for Latin America's indifference to the democratic phase of the libertarian tide. This indifference was already apparent in 1811. "The war of liberation had actually begun to turn into a war between Americans, for no party was prepared to see the other taking the lead in the vacuum, and all were more disposed to admit the Spaniards than to see their fellow citizens in power.... What hampered the whole movement from the very outset, moreover, was the conservatism of the colored population. While in North America freedom had been demanded with passion, and hence quickly won, by a majority of white settlers, here in South America the millions of colored men hung like a dead weight on the small white minority and dragged them down again and again into the apathy of the past." [12]

Bolívar in 1812 lost his fortune and his title simultaneously, and this was the best thing that could have happened to him. A pauper in Curaçao, Jamaica, and Haiti, he was thrown back upon his inner resources to win adherents to his several harebrained "invasions" of the mother country. By the time he had conceived the brilliant idea of using Colombia to seize Venezuela, he had also become adept at rationalizing the uses of naked force, setting up one dictatorship in opposition to another, reconciling himself to the retributive massacre of 870 enemy prisoners—"You have too few men and too many prisoners," he wrote one of his captains, "I therefore command you to have all the Spaniards now in the fortress or in the hospital killed" —designing gaudy uniforms to impress a Spanish-bred people, enlisting England with her rival imperialistic motives to his cause, and proposing a hereditary senate and a lifetime chief executive for Venezuela on the English model.

The two incredible crossings of the Andes between New Granada (Colombia) and Venezuela—the second was called "the most magnificent episode in the history of warfare" by a French military historian a hundred years later—established Bolívar as the foremost contender for power on the continent. Compared to San Martín, he was an amateur soldier, but in the ability to sway men, partly by his electrifying presence and partly by his political imagination—the capacity to make men think, momentarily, in terms larger than them-

[12] Emil Ludwig, *Bolívar: The Life of an Idealist.* New York, Ziff-Davis, 1942. Ludwig does not add that the apathy of the Indians was a state of mind induced, as we have seen, by the force at the disposal of the white minority.

selves, beyond national boundaries—Bolívar had no equal. The super-state larger than Europe that he put together out of Ecuador, New Granada, and Venezuela for a season was to provide the first stage of a continental confederation. Columbus was to give it its name, and (another stroke of genius) "Las Casas" was to be its capital. Un-fortunately Bolívar, while sending San Martín in Lima admonitions about the anachronism of monarchical "forms" for Peru, thought nothing of *acting* like a monarch when it came to imposing on Ec-uador what he thought was good for it. The time for the confronta-tion in Guayaquíl had come.

San Martín and Bolívar Meet

What business did Bolívar have in Peru? He had dreamed of one day planting his standard on the "silver mountain of Potosí," and Peru lay between that mountain and Ecuador. For that matter, what business did he have in Ecuador? He went so far as to have docu-ments forged justifying his presence there. At least in the case of Peru he had heard rumors that San Martín was on the verge of coming to terms with Spain. But here was San Martín coming to meet him to disprove such rumors! What should he do?

No record was kept of the conversations of the two great men, but it is clear that the astute Bolívar overwhelmed the reluctant Protector with honors (including a golden laurel wreath) and prom-ised him so much that whatever counterproposals San Martín had come with stuck in his throat. San Martín was ill when he came, and perhaps the glamour of Bolívar's presence and the adulation the latter was receiving from women gave San Martín a sense of age and in-adequacy. There was a ball in his honor on the night of July 27, 1822. Bolívar is reported to have "danced frantically in a maelstrom of gold braid and décolletés." Presently San Martín slipped out, remarking, "I can't stand this noise." He went aboard the ship on which he had arrived only thirty-six hours before, and set sail for Peru. The egocentric Bolívar sent him a parting gift—his own por-trait!

One month later San Martín wrote Bolívar a letter. He rebuked him gently for the annexation of Ecuador. "I did not believe it behooved us to decide this important matter. At the end of the war the respective governments would have decided it, without the troubles that may now result for the new states of South America." Then, after telling Bolívar of the superiority of the royalist forces still entrenched in Peru, he stated the ostensible reason for the renunciation he was about to make:

> I am deeply convinced that America's independence is irrevocable; but I am also convinced that the prolongation of the war will be the ruin of its peoples, and it is the sacred duty for the men in whose hands lies its destiny to prevent a continuation of such evils . . . I shall embark for Chile. . . . My presence is the only obstacle which prevents you from coming to Peru with the army you command.[13]

Why did San Martín reject Bolívar's offer to serve under his command? Why did San Martín refuse Bolívar's offer of troops to reinforce him against the Spanish? Because their number was inadequate? Was San Martín's poor health the major factor? Or was he tired of hearing the quarrelsome Peruvian criollos call him a tyrant? There was certainly a strong element of neurosis in both great men—San Martín moaning about "my old age" at forty-four; Bolívar's constantly running complaint, "I have reached the end of my career. . . . The presence of a human being makes me ill. . . . From all sides terror invades me, and the noise of falling things. This is the epoch of catastrophes." Was San Martín lacking in will? Was Bolívar lacking in humility? Was San Martín lacking in humor? Was Bolívar too frivolous? As in all tragedies, there was an element of mystery in the denouement. The flaw in each man's character guaranteed that they would not unite; and once they parted there was no chance at all that the Spanish colonies would come together.

From Guayaquíl to Ayacucho

For a year after San Martín's retirement from Peru, Bolívar stalled in Ecuador. If he was waiting for an invitation, he was waiting in vain. The rich criollos in Lima were doing their best to get rid of the incorruptible San Martín; they had no desire to take orders from another *libertador*. Yet the situation was deteriorating. The royalist army was getting stronger. The shell of a government that San Martín had left behind him was getting closer and closer to anarchy. Finally, in September of 1823, Bolívar received grudging "permission" from Gran Colombia to move. He sailed from Guayaquíl for Callao and a few days later entered Lima in triumph. He found the

[13] Quoted in Rojas, *op. cit.* This letter was not released by San Martín until a decade after Bolívar's death. The original was not found among Bolívar's papers.

treasury empty. The governing officials had become peddlers of graft. The provinces were a prey to bandits and smugglers. The acting President was fighting the Congress. The Mayor of Lima presented him with—three pretty girls!

Bolívar set the girls free, dismissed the Mayor, arrested the President, set up an army of Peruvians backboned by his own force and headed by Sucre, sent for his faithful Ecuadorean mistress, and sighed, "I wish I had never seen Peru...." Soon he developed consumption. Only the reports of growing dissension at home, and the thought that the loss of Peru would be followed by the loss of Ecuador and then Colombia, kept him in Lima. But instead of addressing himself to Peru's civil problems, he seems to have abandoned himself to a succession of amatory adventures and left the most urgent problem, the military one, to the able and devoted Sucre.

Sucre was only twenty-nine when Bolívar, after watching him win a preliminary cavalry engagement with the Spanish at Junín on August 6, 1824, turned over command of the poorly equipped army of six thousand men to him. Sucre met the Spanish army of ten thousand superbly armed royalist soldiers on the plain of Ayacucho December 29 and routed them in a battle lasting only seventy minutes. Two thousand Spaniards were slain, the Viceroy and all his generals were captured; the Spanish power in South America was broken forever. Ever generous, Bolívar congratulated Sucre and loaded him with honors, but he was disillusioned when Sucre encouraged Upper Peru to secede and form its own government, and only slightly mollified when the new state was named in his honor, Bolivia. He lingered on in Lima for the better part of another year, hopelessly incapable of bringing order out of the governmental chaos that had disillusioned San Martín. Finally he turned north to try to bring peace to the secession tearing Greater Colombia apart behind his back. "I have come to Colombia," he cried, "to save both you and our country [Venezuela] from the greatest of all catastrophes. No personal ambition brought me here.... I want no throne, no presidency, nothing.... I seek only tranquility for Venezuela so that I may resign my office." [14] It was all true, but it was irrelevant. Colombia, Venezuela, and Ecuador repudiated him and became separate states. Bolívar died a broken man, declaring bitterly that "America is ungovernable." From Mexico to Patagonia the only class that the Spaniards had seen fit to give a small stake in the colonies was abdicating political power to the military.

[14] Quoted in Herring, *op. cit.*

4

NINETEENTH CENTURY:
THE WAR WITH CHILE

THE aimless course of Peru's history in the nineteenth century, culminating in the humiliating disaster of the War of the Pacific, was a consequence of the events just related. The suppression of the Indian majority following the execution of Tupac Amaru II ensured that nothing of the welfare socialism of the Inca system would survive except its ancestral foundation. And the ancestral foundation, without its overall rational plan, provided only an effective means of keeping the Quechua-speaking highlanders in a state of brutish ignorance. The War of Independence, Baudin reminds us, "was not a movement of popular independence by the Indians. . . . It was the large property owners, big business, and the clergy that led the struggle, all of them desiring autonomy above everything else; and it was a 'great aristocrat,' Bolívar, who triumphed."

It need not have been so. But Bolívar's personality, as we have seen, was in conflict with his ideals. Though he had said repeatedly that "principles are the guarantee of civil rights," that "spiritual morality is the law of conscience," and that every "prescription robs faith of its merit," he compromised with his constitution for Peru, permitting the foundation of a Catholic state. Bolívar's ambivalence vis-à-vis the Indians was even more fatal. He who had called Las Casas "the apostle of America," and fulminated (in Venezuela) against "the national ferocity of the Spanish character," [1] confessed in Peru that he dreaded nothing so much as the departure of the last Spaniard. And the guilt that he must have felt for this distrust of the

[1] Quoted in Lewis Hanke, *Bartolomé de las Casas: Bookman, Scholar, Propagandist.* Philadelphia, University of Pennsylvania Press, 1952.

58

criollo he buried under grandiose plans for the regeneration of the continent—which in turn negated the democratic fervor with which he had liberated the northern states. "I have twenty-two thousand unoccupied soldiers," he mused on the way to Potosí; "if the Argentine were threatened by Brazil, it would be a good opportunity and a glorious affair. I might become dictator of America." And to his deputy in the north he wrote: "Believe me, Chile is lost without me. If I remain in the south, I could come to Colombia's help from here with twenty thousand men. In a word, all is lost if I leave here. Demand the consent of Congress to my remaining in Peru." [2]

But the criollos of Peru, as we have seen, were only too glad to get rid of Bolívar, whose fitful idealism might at any moment interfere with their plans to continue the exploitation of Peru's riches. A cynical priest in Lima had anticipated their impatience in this rhyme:

> When at Ayacucho, we
> broke our fetters with Spain,
> it was no more than the swapping
> of a dirty nose for a drooling mouth.
> Yes, we changed our condition,
> passed from the power of Don Fernando [Ferdinand VII]
> into the hands of Don Simón. [3]

The Marshals of Ayacucho Seize the Spoils

The Battle of Ayacucho did more than break the power of Spain. It provided Peru with a pride of contentious lions. These self-styled field marshals kept the new nation in a state of boiling anarchy until the dictatorship of one of them, Ramón Castilla (1845-62), provided an interim of order before the deluge.

No sooner had Bolívar's Colombian brigade embarked in March of 1827 than General Andrés Santa Cruz, a mestizo descended on his mother's side from the Incas, made himself President of the Council of Government and proceeded to abolish the Liberator's mildly liberal constitution. His rapacious colleagues, Gen. José de Lamar, who had commanded the Peruvian Legion at Ayacucho, and

[2] Quoted in Emil Ludwig, *Bolívar: The Life of an Idealist*. New York, Ziff-Davis, 1942.
[3] Cited in Jorge Basadre's *Historia de la Republica del Peru*, Lima, 1946. Translated in Hubert Herring, *A History of Latin America*. New York, Alfred A. Knopf, Inc., 1955.

Gen. Agustín Gamarra, the Legion's chief of staff, saw another threat of liberalism in the presence in Bolivia of the noble Sucre, recently elected President-for-life of that unhappy country. They went after him. Sucre was forced to resign and sail from Arica to Guayaquil, and on January 1, 1829, Santa Cruz took over in La Paz, where he holed up for a decade, threatening every gesture toward stability in neighboring Peru. Sucre won his last victory a month later, defeating Lamar in Ecuador. The victor of Ayacucho (still only thirty-five) was assassinated on his way to Quito in June 1830. Shortly thereafter Lamar was seized in Piura by Gamarra and exiled to Central America.

There now ensued in Lima a struggle for power between the despotic Gamarra and Gen. Luis José Orbegoso, a rich planter of Trujillo. Orbegoso won a narrow convention victory for the presidency, but Gamarra's troops forced him to flee with his ousted convention to Callao. Gamarra's troops deserted him, however, and soon Orbegoso was reentering Lima in triumph. The game of musical chairs now accelerated. On November 9, 1834, Orbegoso marched south to put down a rebellion. Felipe Santiago de Salaverry, a handsome six-foot-two twenty-eight-year-old officer of Ayacucho who was of pure Basque descent and had much of Bolívar's idealism and charisma, had been entrusted by Orbegoso with the pursuit of Gamarra. Suddenly the young lion returned to Lima to put down a rebellion that had taken place there in his chief's absence; inebriated with his success in taking Callao's fortress by storm, he promptly declared that *he* was now Peru's legitimate President! Salaverry, as Markham sizes him up, "knew what was right but his life was a series of actions against his better judgment. His career explains the history of his country for twenty years after the independence. It was a nation of Salaverrys." [4]

Only the city of Arequipa in the south failed to declare for Salaverry. But there the young poetry-writing Marshal whose motto was, "We must seek danger!" was fated to come to grief. It began when Santa Cruz, making a deal with Orbegoso, marched out of Bolivia into southern Peru and took Cuzco from Gamarra. Salaverry rushed south and managed to seize rebellious Arequipa, but no sooner had he left Lima when mounted Negro bandits from the coast seized the capital briefly and cut off his reinforcements. General Miller (acting for Santa Cruz) defeated Salaverry, and over

[4] Sir Clements Markham, *A History of Peru.* Chicago, 1892.

Miller's protests Santa Cruz had him shot with all his staff in the great square of the southern capital.

Santa Cruz was now at last in a position to quit his Bolivian stronghold and attempt to reunite the whole of the ancient viceroyalty. A vain, cruel man but an able ruler, he staked everything on bringing Ecuador, Peru, and Bolivia together again—and lost. He lost because his execution of Salaverry had alienated the people in the one part of the country he needed most, the part bordering on Chile. Chile, it should be noted, was no longer the country it had been under its liberal liberator, Bernardo O'Higgins. O'Higgins had been driven out by a reactionary oligarchy, and this oligarchy was already eyeing greedily the mineral-rich provinces across the narrow nation's northern border. On the pretext that Peru had declared Arica a free port, thus threatening Chile's vital Pacific trade, the Chilean Navy on August 21, 1836, seized Peru's warships in the harbor serving Tacna. When the Chileans next landed troops at Ancón, north of Lima, Santa Cruz evacuated the capital and retreated into the Callejón de Huaylas (*see* pp. 146–148). There, at the Pan de Azúcar, near Yunguay, the troops of the short-lived confederation were routed. Santa Cruz escaped to Europe. His mildly liberal constitution was abolished by a convention at Huancayo with only two dissenting votes. The Chileans, glad to have the merger of the three states ended, and the reactionary Gamarra back in power, departed.

Other than the Chileans, however, no one wanted Gamarra. The Bolivians touched off the inevitable revolt. A Bolivian army defeated Gamarra at Ingavi and then invaded Peru, where civil war was raging. Order was restored only briefly in 1843, when Gen. Agostín Vivanco, one of the last of the men of Ayacucho, took Lima—while his wife, emulating Bolívar's warlike mistress Manuela Sáenz, was taking Arequipa.

Marshal Castilla Restores Order

The last, and by all odds the ablest, of the staff officers who had served under Sucre in the famous battle was Ramón Castilla. Born a mestizo in 1797, Castilla had been twenty-seven at Ayacucho but already a veteran. As a cadet of nineteen in the royalist army opposing San Martín in Chile, he had been taken prisoner at Chacabuco. At Yunguay he commanded the cavalry. At Ingavi, fighting for Gamarra, he had been taken prisoner again and was being held in

La Paz when Bolivia was invaded. A small man with bright fierce eyes under beetling brows and a projecting lower lip, he had already gained a reputation for being masterful yet forgiving, conservative but flexible enough to initiate minimal reforms.

Whether it was because his wife was an Arequipeño and he himself had been born still farther to the south, at Tarapacá, or whether these geographical facts of birth were merely coincidental, Castilla's twenty-year domination of Peruvian politics had its solid economic base in the extraordinary fertilizer boom concentrated in that part of the country. It began, even before the revelation of nitrate deposits in the Atacama Desert, with a rediscovery of nitrogen-rich guano on the uninhabited offshore islands. The use and canny conservation of this prosaic treasure by the Incas has already been mentioned. Humboldt had made references to the fertilizing properties of these deposits of bird dung in the early 1800's. But it was not until the early 1840's that the proud Spanish-speaking possessors got around to doing anything about guano, and then, characteristically, they did the wrong thing. Between 1848 and 1875 they *exported* more than twenty million tons of the precious fertilizer from Peru. Had it been used, as the Incas used it, to increase the common bounty, Peru would have become a rich agricultural country again. Instead, only two things were accomplished. A new class of "guano millionaires" was created—Castilla's backers; and the guano deposits were exhausted. To be sure, Castilla had made both guano and nitrate state monopolies, but this only meant that the enormous profits were divided between the bureaucracy and the contractors and shippers Castilla chose to license. This arrangement worked well enough for the "in" group; but in the case of nitrate, where Peru lacked engineers and capital for strip-mining, the way was prepared for the disaster of 1879. Castilla entrusted the deposits of his native Tarapacá to British concessionaires in league with the land-hungry Chileans.

Castilla's twenty-year dictatorship is still looked back upon by Peruvians as something of a golden age, and the fierce but relatively benevolent Marshal is regarded as one of the nation's heroes. His constitution of 1860 (Peru's fifteenth since Bolívar) concentrated the presidential power and severely restricted the franchise. His admirers claim that he ended forced tribute by the Indians, abolished Negro slavery, did away with Church courts and tithes, built schools. It is true that the astute dictator made these and other concessions to the liberals, but none of these reforms substantially improved the lot of the beneficiaries. The Indians and Negroes were induced to give Castilla grudging support,[5] but they continued to be imposed upon by other means.

Taxation, for example, continued much as it always had. The last viceroys, in an effort to dampen the smoldering fires of Indian resentment, had changed the name of the traditional tribute every Indian had to pay to *contribución de indígenas*. This forced contribution, which Kubler calls "essentially a tax on biological existence," was continued intact under the Republic. The Republicans *claimed* to be taxing the entire nation for the first time, regardless of class, but the three additional taxes levied on the castas were never properly collected, and efforts to collect them invariably resulted in "changes" at the top. "Each new usurper was likely to abolish the tax to gain popular favor. And each new usurper collected the tax surreptitiously until the new form of the old law was again promulgated." Castilla was able to gain Indian support by officially abolishing the hated contribución in 1854 because the sudden wealth from guano was filling the treasury to overflowing. But the tax continued to be exacted in some provinces illegally anyway, and when the guano bonanza had run its course, other means were found to make the Indians pay, as they always had, for the state's deficits.

The clerical reforms didn't go far enough to antagonize or weaken the Church, but it kept the anticlericals quiet. The few schools built were showpieces; the big money went into roads, telegraph lines, and servicing the public debt. To the armed forces went only enough to ensure the policing of existing boundaries. The ease with which Castilla had defeated Vivanco at Carmen Alta in 1843 may have made the Marshal sanguine about Peru's security. Yet the ease with which he himself was able to mount a successful revolt against his own puppet, José Rufino Echenique, in 1855, when the latter had proved himself unpopular and corrupt, might have given the grizzled commander pause.

After the Battle of La Palma in that year Castilla was again elected constitutional President. He had his two emancipation proclamations confirmed by the rubber-stamp Congress. Two years later Vivanco made another bid for power, encouraged by Chile and by a mutiny

[5] How grudging may be guessed from the following passage in Peruvian novelist Ciro Alegría's *Broad and Alien Is the World*, translated by Harriet de Onís. (Chester Springs, Pennsylvania, Dufour Editions, 1963): "It is told of Marshal Castilla that whenever he heard an Indian humming to himself, he said: 'An Indian who sings the songs of his region is surely a deserter. Give him forty lashes.'"

of the southern naval squadron, but again the ease with which Castilla managed to run the fleet gauntlet and recapture Arica from the rebels served to give Peru a false sense of security. In 1858 there was another unsuccessful attempt to impose Peru's will upon Ecuador —lost, it will be recalled, since Bolívar's hasty retreat back across the Andes. From 1860 until his death in 1867 Castilla was occupied with the problem of the succession. Marshals del Mar, San Román, and Pezet, all men of Ayacucho, were given trial runs, and it was during the presidency of the upright and fairly able Juan Antonio Pezet (1863–65) that Spain, abetted by Chile, made a last futile attempt to regain a foothold on the continent. Chile, when Spain finally turned against her and shelled Valparaiso, took the lessons to heart: she began building a modern war fleet.

Henry Meiggs and the Great Railroad Boom

In the twelve years that remained to be frittered away between the death of Marshal Castilla and the calamity of 1879, the increasingly chaotic Peruvian stage was dominated by an eloquent, unscrupulous American contractor, Henry Meiggs, whose "success" in selling Peru a railroad system (the last thing it needed) guaranteed the debacle; and by a noble native son, Manuel Pardo, the best and least-appreciated President Peru had had, who failed against impossible odds to save his bankrupt country.

Marx once revised Hegel thus: Great events and personalities *do* recur on the stage of history, but for the second time not as tragedy but as farce. San Martín's renunciation of Peru was tragic. But when President Pezet sailed for England in 1865 to "save" Peru from civil war, his renunciation, however well meant, was both unnecessary and irrelevant. His own Vice President, Pedro Diez Canseco, had joined Mariano Ignacio Prado, and under cover of the confusion caused by Spain's seizure of the Chincha Islands and Admiral Parejo's ill-advised attack upon the Chilean squadron to the south, the two would-be *caudillos* were marching on Lima. The revolt could have been suppressed if Pezet had attended to business, but instead Prado was enabled to make himself dictator and come to terms with Chile. The disgruntled Diez Canseco could now pose as a legitimist so effectively that the old Marshal Castilla himself was induced to return from exile in Europe in his aid, landing at Tarapacá only to die pathetically by the roadside a few days later. Prado was overthrown anyway, the insurrection of the palace guard being led by Col. José

Balta, and Diez Canseco became provisional President until August 2, 1868, when Balta was elected to succeed him. The great railroad-building spree had already begun.

It was Diez Canseco who persuaded "Enrique" Meiggs that the fortune he was making building railroads for Chile would be as nothing to what awaited him in Peru. And Balta emptied the treasury to pay the bill. It began modestly enough when Diez Canseco, a proud Arequipeño, thought it would be nice to connect his lovely city with the port of Mollendo. No sooner was this project under way when someone (Meiggs?) conceived the brilliant idea of running a huge iron pipe discharging 433,000 gallons of fresh water every twenty-four hours the whole eighty-five miles from the seven-thousand-foot-high city to the hot, salty port. The Arequipa railway was built with great dispatch (nine months instead of the three years Meiggs had estimated) and was opened in January of 1871. But politicians in Cuzco and Puno, far to the north and east, saw no reason why their cities shouldn't share in the bonanza. The Puno spur alone cost £4,346,659, the rest of the southern system somewhat more than double that sum. But Meiggs was just beginning to sense the possibilities when Balta took over from Diez Canseco and told him that the sky (literally) was to be the limit. *Every* coastal river valley in Peru should be the terminus of a trans-Andean railway. One, from Chimbote to Huallanca in the Callejón de Huaylas, was actually built. Another (*see* pp. 149–150) was sent to start from Callao and Lima and terminate at Cerro de Pasco and Huancayo after cutting through the 15,693-foot pass at Galera. Here, in its final tunnel, it would become the highest railway in the world. Meiggs told Balta that the cost of this line (it was not to be completed for decades) would be another five million pounds.

Balta was not at all alarmed. The £37,000,000 of railways he had now ordered from the jolly, optimistic Meiggs constituted only a fraction of the public works the President now set about spawning. The port of Callao was widened and dredged. Pisco was given an iron pier. The tributaries of the Amazon—the Perené as far as Tarma, the Huallaga to Yurimaguas—were explored with a view to giving Peru an outlet for its trade on the Atlantic. The Amazon settlement of Iquitos (*see* pp. 173–181), destined to bring this dream to reality in less than half a century, was founded.

As for Meiggs, "From the President of the Republic on down," a contemporary Peruvian witness noted, "he counted the most trusted officials among his boughten minions, and the besotted people went mad with cheering while their ruin was being purchased with their own gold." [6] Meiggs can hardly be blamed for the existing corruption, nor for the willingness of Peru's politicians to squander Peru's financial resources on building railroads rather than on public welfare or defense. It can only be said that his presence was the catalytic agent for a bubble that was bound to expand until it burst. With a minimum amount of investigation, Diez Canseco and Balta could have ascertained that "Honest Harry," before coming to Chile, had been forced to flee San Francisco, one step ahead of the police who had discovered the forgeries with which he had attempted to hide the bankruptcy of his first building venture. In Chile, Meiggs appears to have contracted for the railroads efficiently and with a minimum of padding; either he found that bribes there were frowned upon or unnecessary. But in Peru he did what everybody else was doing. ("Here in this country," Bolívar had remarked, "no one can live. There are too many crooks.") Every contract in Peru contained provisions for bribery of government officials—some running into the millions. To ensure a plentiful supply of cheap labor, Meiggs imported Chinese coolies by the shipload—many of them dying of soroche in the high passes. When the country went bankrupt in 1876, three years before the Chilean invasion, "Don Enrique" went bankrupt with it, dying a pauper in that year with only 87 of the 138 miles of the Oroya skyway laid down.

As for Balta, the first President of Peru who was not a Man of Ayacucho, he was great in energy and ambition only. Two weaknesses undid him. Increasing the public debt from £3,800,000 to £49,000,000 meant negotiating loans with an annual *interest* of £2,500,000—payment of which left Peru's treasury empty. Balta's second mistake was distributing colonelcies in the army to worthless relations like the Gutiérrez clan. Tomás Gutiérrez was Minister of War in 1872 when Manuel Pardo, the candidate of the new Civilista Party that was trying to save Peru from its militarists, received the vote of the electors to succeed Balta. Balta first tried to use Gutiérrez to terrorize the electors into selecting another military man, but then thought better of it. As a result Gutiérrez murdered him, and Pardo sought asylum aboard the battleship *Huáscar* in Callao Harbor. The Lima mob then lynched the Gutiérrez brothers —Tomás cowering in his bathtub like Marat before his head was bashed in with a whisky bottle. The bodies were burned in the Cathedral square. "It was," says a contemporary witness who sounds

[6] Quoted in Watt Stewart, *Henry Meiggs, Yankee Pizarro.* Durham, North Carolina, Duke University Press, 1946.

as though he must have seen many such scenes, "the best behaved crowd before such a spectacle that I ever saw in my life." [7] The times were now overprepared for a man of principle.

Manuel Pardo Tries to Save Peru

If ever there was a prophet and good man without honor in his own country, it was Manuel Pardo. Even today Pardo is not recognized in Peru for what he was. Castilla the autocrat, Piérola the romantic rascal, even the brutal treasure hunter Pizarro, all have their monuments, but Pardo, for reasons which may already be implicit in this narrative but which will be discussed more fully in the next chapter, has still to become a hero in the country he exerted unfailing wisdom to save.

The first civilian to become President, Manuel Pardo was thrifty, phlegmatic, and practical—qualities not exactly deified in the Spanish pantheon, and a complete anomaly in Peru. Only the fact of his ancient criollo lineage made him tolerated at all. In experience he was already rich. As Minister of Hacienda under the dictator Prado he had reformed the thief-infested customs, abolished pawnshops, eliminated featherbedding in the inspection services, suppressed unlawful pensions—all of which had made him respected if not popular. He had also proposed stabilizing the country's credit by the truly revolutionary means of taxing landowners and heavily assessing the exports of cotton and minerals. Needless to say, Pardo had been forced out; and while Balta and his Finance Minister Nicolás de Piérola were completing the bankruptcy of the country, Pardo had quietly organized his own party, the Civilistas, and written tracts to prepare public opinion for a rational use of Peru's great resources. One of these, *Estudios sobre la Provincia de Jauja* (1862), is prophetic indeed. Anticipating Fernando Belaúnde Terry's program a century later, it suggested that the *eastern slopes* of the Andes be connected to the proposed railway system with access roads and that the Amazon tributaries be controlled to deny Brazil the profits already slipping out of Peru along the Amazon to the Atlantic. Although the Civilista program was firmly opposed to government by the military, Pardo believed in a strong army, and his own record as a patriot was unimpeachable. During the bombardment of Callao by the Spanish fleet in May of 1866 he had personally manned a shore battery, and had tended the wounded. The grateful people of

[7] Thomas J. Hutchinson, *Two Years in Peru, with Explorations of Its Antiquities.* 2 vols. London, 1873.

Lima had given him a medal in 1869 for his humanity and philanthropy during the yellow-plague epidemic the year before, and had followed this up by electing him Mayor.

No man was ever better prepared for the presidency than Manuel Pardo, and no man came to the office at a worse time or received less support. Diplomatically he named a general as his Prime Minister, and then went to work. He cut waste. He increased taxes. He tried to meet payments on the huge national debt. He invited technical experts to Peru. And all this he did without the familiar dictatorial steamroller that had flattened opposition in the past. He even found time to have the first census taken, to establish an engineering school, to inaugurate a badly needed political science department at the University, to encourage literature and the arts, and to make alliances designed to hold off the threat from Chile. But what Pardo had to contend with is summed up by Professor Owens:

> It was a heavy program even granted stable conditions, but, to add to his difficulties, his four years of office were punctuated by great disturbances and intrigues, including attempts on his life. His chief enemy was the founder of the ultramontane right-wing Democratic Party, Nicolás de Piérola. . . . While Pardo wished for power in order to legislate reform, Piérola merely wished for power. Their common quality was organizing ability, but they never really understood one another, and the conflict between their parties stemmed from a personal antipathy. Piérola, like Castilla, saw himself as the messiah and saviour of his country, and he was quite prepared, when revolution failed, to try assassination.[8]

The Civilista movement's understandable desire not to antagonize the military led to its undoing—and Manuel Pardo's. When its candidate for the 1876 election died, Gen. Mariano Ignacio Prado, the dictator who had succeeded Pezet in 1865, was selected in the hope that he would reconcile the pro- and anti-militarists. Pardo supported him reluctantly. Not surprisingly, Prado sided with the army politicians, and Pardo was obliged to flee the country. Returning to preside over the Senate in 1878, he was assassinated on the eve of the calamity he had done so much to head off.

[8] R. J. Owens, *Peru.* Oxford University Press, 1963.

Peru and the War of the Pacific: 1879–83

It will be recalled that Chile, with British backing, had been taking advantage of the instability of Peru and Bolivia to penetrate deeper and deeper into the nitrate deposits of the Atacama Desert. This wasteland spilled over into the southernmost Peruvian provinces of Tacna and Arica, containing the cities with the same names. The province of Atacama, whose capital was Antofagasta, was part of Bolivia; and Antofagasta was that otherwise landlocked country's principal seaport. The boundaries were ill defined, since the whole area was thought valueless at the time they were drawn. As the Chilean-British prospectors began to find rich deposits of nitrate farther and farther north, the boundaries were subtly redefined to include them. In 1873 Peru, as worried as was Bolivia about this steady encroachment, concluded a secret treaty of defense with Bolivia. But the following year Chile got Bolivia to agree not to raise export duties in the area or to otherwise penalize Chilean capital. Two years later Peru moved to protect itself by expropriating nitrate concessionaires, mostly Chilean, in Tarapacá. In 1878, hoping to take advantage of a border dispute between Chile and Argentina, Bolivia canceled its similar concession to the Chilean-British nitrate combine in Antofagasta. At once Chile seized Antofagasta and points north. Bolivia declared war on Chile. Peru tried to mediate, but Chile demanded that she denounce the (no longer secret) treaty of 1873 with Bolivia, and when Peru refused, declared war on her too. It was April 5, 1879.[9]

How little anyone in Peru suspected the virulence of the enemy's intentions is shown by the fact that Pardo and Piérola, patriots both, however bitterly opposed to one another, had sought refuge in Chile in 1877. Piérola had fled Peru after attempting to unseat Pardo's successor, Mariano Ignacio Prado, by seizing the armor-plated cruiser *Huáscar* in Callao Harbor. If he got wind in Chile of the powerful ironclads being built for that country in England—each of them capable of firing explosive shells through the thin armor plate of such obsolete vessels as the *Huáscar* and the *Independencia* —it was much too late to do anything about it. Pardo sounded warnings on his return to Peru but was not heeded. One of Chile's formidable new cruisers was appropriately named after the gentle-

[9] Owens, *op. cit.*, pp. 47–48.

man who had looted Peru's treasury in 1822, the *Almirante Cochrane*.

The *Huáscar*, nevertheless, provided Peru with her only bright chapter in the war—the first chapter. Her commander, Miguel Grau, was a son of one of Sucre's captains at Ayacucho. In the harbor of Iquique, south of Arica, where Peru's Army was assembling to repel invasion, Grau managed to ram and sink the blockading Chilean corvette *Esmeralda*. In the long run, Peru's loss of the *Independencia*, which ran on the rocks in the same engagement, proved costlier; but for six months Grau now harassed the coastline, preventing invasion of Peru by sea, and even occasionally raiding Chilean ports. Grau was finally trapped, along with a second ship, the *Unión*, off Antofagasta. He died when a shell exploded inside the conning tower; but his fight to the death permitted the faster *Unión* to escape, and he became the first of the heroes of this lost war whose monuments now dot Peru's cities.

Peru's only land victory, a Pyrrhic one, came after the landing of a small army at Tarapacá. Why, instead of pursuing the defeated Chileans, the victorious Peruvians and Bolivians retreated, has never been clear. At nearby Tacna 9,000 of the allies held off 14,000 Chileans, but with a disastrous toll of 2,128 dead. In Lima, meanwhile, discouraged by the loss of the *Huáscar* and now the whole province of Tarapacá, President Prado suddenly abandoned his post. It was announced that he had gone to England to buy ironclads! Piérola, seeing his chance, seized the government and organized a spirited defense of Callao against the Chilean fleet. But with only one vessel, the *Unión*, now remaining, the odds were hopeless. On May 10, 1880, hundreds of projectiles were lobbed into Lima.

In the south the Chilean Army advanced relentlessly upon Arica. The remnant of the Peruvian Army, now commanded by Col. Francisco Bolognesi, who had distinguished himself at Tarapacá, refused to surrender the city. The forts were carried by assault and the garrison of six hundred was massacred, but Peru had two more dead heroes—the gallant Bolognesi, who had telegraphed that he intended to "fight to the last cartridge," and Alfonso Ugarte, a wealthy young native of Tarapacá serving on Bolognesi's staff, who (legend has it) rode his horse over a cliff into the Pacific rather than surrender the flag. According to the United States Minister in Arica, "the Chileans behaved like savages, murdering the wounded. . . . It was not war but wholesale murder." [10] Nevertheless Chile now controlled all of

[10] Quoted in Sir Clements Markham's *The War Between Chile and Peru: 1879–1882*, published in London in 1883, a highly partisan account of what happened here and in Lima from the Peruvian point of view.

Bolivia's maritime province and the southern provinces of Peru as well.

For several months Peru's long coastline, from Arica to Tumbes, was systematically raided and looted by Adm. Patricio Lynch. This served to cripple industry and communications in the river valleys. Then a Chilean army of thirty thousand men under the command of Gen. Manuel Baquedano was landed to take the capital in a pincers, one force marching north from Pisco, the other descending from Curayaco. Piérola organized all males from sixteen to sixty in defense of the capital (which then had a population of a hundred thousand), but with the Army gone and weapons scarce, this motley force was no match for the attackers with their four-thousand-yard-range Krupp artillery. All of Peru's remaining ships were sunk in Callao Harbor. In a battle in the suburb of Chorrillos four thousand Peruvians fell, half as many Chileans. Another suburb, Miraflores, was stoutly defended by Andrés Cáceres, but it succumbed too, and was burned. The surrounding villas were sacked, and only a firm stand by the diplomatic corps prevented the burning of Lima, which fell to the Chileans.[11]

Piérola assembled a rump Congress at Arequipa and then escaped to Europe. García Calderón was permitted to set up a government in Lima, but in the midst of mediation efforts the Chileans packed him off to Valparaiso. Adm. Lizardo Montero and Gen. Miguel Iglesias served briefly as Presidents, but the occupation forces were giving the orders, and only Andrés Cáceres in the Jauja Valley was still holding the Chileans at bay.

Lima was occupied for two years and nine months, a traumatic experience from which Peru still bears psychological scars. Lynch is said to have removed three thousand wagonloads of household belongings and art treasures from Chorrillos alone. The University of San Marcos and the great library were turned into barracks. Price-

[11] According to a Chilean historian (Luis Galdames in *A History of Chile*, Chapel Hill, North Carolina, University of North Carolina Press, 1941), Lima and Callao were sacked by their own populace during Piérola's defense. "It was therefore necessary for the Chilean Army to make a hurried entrance into these cities in order to prevent the rabble from continuing its pillage." From the Chilean point of view, it is only fair to add, the war was touched off by Bolivia's flagrant disregard of the Treaty of 1874 and by Peru's greed for nitrates, which led to the secret Peru-Bolivia alliance. Galdames claims that the "entire population" of Antofagasta welcomed the Chileans as liberators, that the naval hero of Iquique was not Grau but Arturo Prat, whose wooden ships stood up to Grau's armored ones, and that after the Battle of Arica England offered to mediate "but Peru refused." A neutral account of this war has never been written—and probably couldn't be: the sources in all three countries were too emotionally inflamed.

less books and manuscripts were thrown into the streets. In Miraflores Ricardo Palma's collection of manuscripts was burned. The occupation lasted so long not because Chile's able war President, Aníbal Pinto, was not trying to withdraw but because no Peruvian government willing to surrender Peruvian territory could be found. Finally such a government was shaken together, and in the Treaty of Ancón (1884) Iglesias bowed to the inevitable and ceded Tarapacá Province permanently, the cities of Tacna and Arica for ten years. It was not until 1929, however, and then through American mediation, that Chile finally evacuated Tacna (*see* pp. 168–169) and conceded Peru a customs wharf and railway station in Arica. Bolivia, of course, lost her entire seacoast—a state of affairs that still rankles and at La Paz is denounced in annual street demonstrations.

Aftermath: Cáceres and Piérola

It was inevitable that the signer of the humiliating peace would receive the backlash of popular frustration, and it was also inevitable that General Cáceres, who alone had held out against the Chilean arms, would achieve the presidency. Cáceres and his Constitutionalist Party, followed by Cáceres' chosen successor, Morales Bermúdez, were in power from 1886 to 1894, and order was restored without any significant reforms.

The significant event of this period was the arrangement under which the bankrupt, war-ravaged country was bailed out by foreign creditors who received in return virtual control over Peru's trade. The arrangement was drawn up by two Americans, W. R. and Michael Grace. In 1890 the resulting Peruvian Corporation was incorporated in London. It assumed the whole external debt of Peru (£50,000,000), in exchange for which Peru ceded control over its railways and gave a lien on three million tons of guano—both concessions to run for sixty-six years. The corporation was also given management of the steamship line on Lake Titicaca (*see* pp. 163–164), the free use of seven ports, and a cash subsidy of £80,000,000 to be paid in tenths over a thirty-three-year period. Michael Grace, who had earlier received a concession to operate the rich Cerro de Pasco mines, turned this concession over to the Peruvian Corporation. The London banking group also assumed control over the rich deposits of oil which had just been discovered in Talara on the northern coast.

Under the circumstances, the Peruvian Corporation was a good arrangement for Peru, enabling her to concentrate her resources on developing agriculture and industry without the danger of armed intervention by creditors from abroad; but hypersensitivity to later "imperialisms," some real and some fancied, had its roots in this sweeping arrangement.

At the close of Bermúdez' legal term, when Cáceres attempted to dictate another successor, the opposition parties—Democrats (Piérola), Liberals (Durand), and Civilists—united in opposition to Cáceres. A revolutionary army seized the southern provinces and marched on Lima. A fierce battle, with 2,800 casualties on both sides, took place, and Cáceres was defeated. On September 8, 1895, Nicolás de Piérola was once again elected President for a four-year term.

Piérola's administration was uninterrupted this time, save for skirmishes in the remote provinces. Only minor reforms, in the election process and marriage contracts, were made. But the polarization of politics between Piérola's Democrats and the Civilists made for a healthy climate. (Coalitions of these two parties, in fact, ruled for the next thirty-five years.) Piérola with his gaudy uniforms and parades was a popular figure. He called himself "Protector of the Indian," but nothing was done to change the Indian's condition. Both parties represented the land-owning and professional classes exclusively. And as the old boom in guano and nitrate was succeeded by new booms in cotton, sugar, and petroleum, the millionaires of the coastal valleys discovered that they could rule more efficiently without the military. There was even room for a small party of genuine radical dissent. The philosophical anarchist, Manuel González Prada (1848–1918), was permitted to organize, and his anticlerical, anticolonialist, and pro-Indian views helped prepare the way for Haya de la Torre's APRA movement in the 1920's.

In 1899 Piérola was succeeded by Eduardo López de la Romaña, an engineer who had been educated in England. It was a term marked by growing prosperity, the failure to get Chile to withdraw from the provinces of Tacna and Arica, and inconclusive border disputes with Ecuador and Colombia. Manuel Candamo succeeded Romaña in 1903 but died the following year. José Pardo y Barreda, son of the great Manuel, and heir to what little was left of Civilismo, occupied the presidential chair from 1904 to 1908, in which year the commanding figure of Augusto Leguía appeared upon the scene and the history of Peru in the twentieth century may fairly be said to begin.

5

PERU TODAY: LEGUÍA, HAYA DE LA TORRE, ODRÍA, BELAÚNDE

AT first glance the political pattern of twentieth-century Peru may seem no more than an extension of the chaos of the nineteenth century. Civilists and Democrats are at each others' throats still. "Pardos" and "Prados" go on succeeding one another with a confusion not altogether nominal. The military, generally behind the scenes but sometimes openly, still have the last word. The Indians in the highlands remain outside society. The rich get richer, and the poor, constantly increasing in numbers as well as in poverty, ring the flourishing coastal cities.

Actually, the changes taking place beneath this disorderly surface are great. The rise of a small but energetic middle class, finding its voice among the students and faculties of the universities, becomes the catalytic agent. Long before the emergence of political parties expressing the middle class's dissent, Manuel González Prada, the prophetic intellectual, had described the meaninglessness of the voter's choice between Civilists and Democrats as a bumpy walk down a narrow alley smeared with mud and blood. The anticlerical revolution of the landless that Prada—and later the Marxist José Carlos Mariátegui (1895–1930)—was looking for never took place. But the radicals did succeed in bringing about a polarization between "realists" and "idealists." Bearing in mind that *every* government in twentieth-century Peru has had at least the tacit support of the oligarchy, the military establishment, and the Church, the

74

realists industrialized Peru, rebuilt its cities, and brought prosperity to the commercial classes by means of naked dictatorship. The idealists, more often out of power than in, thought in terms of Indian regeneration, labor reforms, planning in national and international configurations, and through their unremitting agitation forced the realists to make important concessions. The realists made their outstanding achievements during the dictatorships of Leguía (1919–30) and Odría (1948–56). The idealists, led by Haya de la Torre, who never actually achieved the presidency, strongly influenced these four decades; and in the person of President Belaúnde they are presently engaged in the attempt to liberalize the face of Peru without drastically altering its class structure.

The Road to Despotism

The appearance on the political scene of Augusto Bernardino Leguía coincided with the demise of Piérola and his Democrat-Civilianist coalition. In his last years in office Piérola had gone a long way to meeting the liberal demands of his Civilista allies, broadening the suffrage to include literate adult males, substituting national conscription for forced recruitment into the armed services, establishing some nonclerical schools, permitting considerable freedom of press. It was a period of intellectual ferment and some prosperity. And the trend away from militarism and toward democracy continued under Piérola's handpicked successor, Eduardo de Romaña (1899–1903), and throughout the two progressive administrations— (1904–08) and (1915–19)—of Manuel Pardo's able son, José.

José Pardo extended education as no other President had, doubling the number of schools and bringing at least some measure of trained competence to 168,000 Peruvians—a pitifully small number, but a beginning. Copper mining at Cerro de Pasco and sugar and cotton production along the coast prospered during Pardo's first term, and it was a hopeful sign that the number of landholders steadily increased. But the coincidence of his second term with World War I brought a cycle of depressions and booms that proved unmanageable, and the scandalous exploitation of rubber in the Amazon Basin (*see* pp. 174–176), already beyond Lima's control, cast a dark shadow. Nevertheless Pardo never wavered from his liberal course. He met the demands of the rising labor movement by limiting hours of work. He forced planters to pay their peons in cash. He created a much-needed agricultural bank for the Indians. He authorized religious toleration. By eradicating yellow fever and malaria, he even managed to lower Peru's fearful death rate.[1]

It was during Pardo's first term that Leguía rose to prominence as Minister of Finance, and it was during the interim between the two Pardo terms that he was first elected President. It was by this time so routine that a Civilist Party candidate be elected that the Democrats under the aged Piérola felt compelled to stage their last two coups, charging military complicity and bribery of the small electorate. The first coup failed, and in the denouement Leguía enhanced his reputation for shrewdness. Examining the resignation which the Piérolistas were demanding that he sign at gunpoint in the great square, he pointed out to them that the document was incorrectly dated; while his enemies were pondering this fine legal point, the President's cavalry dashed in, Leguía dropped to the ground, and by the time he emerged unscathed from under the pile of bodies, the revolution was over. The second revolt, touched off by Leguía's attempt to name a Civilianist successor in 1912, succeeded. Leguía traveled to London, where, during the administration of Guillermo Billinghurst and José Pardo's second term, he successfully recouped his personal fortune.

Considering the fact that Leguía had accomplished little or nothing in the presidency, and that only his reputation for financial acumen—and unfailing luck at the racetrack—was secure, it is surprising that the Civilianists chose him to be their standard-bearer again in 1919. But they did, and apparently Leguía had meditated deeply while in exile about what to do the second time around.

The Dictatorship of Leguía

Even before he was in office, he showed his hand. The Supreme Court was making a routine examination of the election returns. There was no doubt that Leguía had won, but he was taking no chances. In a bloodless coup, Pardo was seized and sent into exile. Leguía took office ahead of schedule and at once set to work to abolish the constitutionalist government he had already begun to undermine in 1912. The lame excuse was that Pardo had been in conspiracy with Congress and the Supreme Court to thwart Leguía's taking office legitimately. The real motive was his fear that once in office, Pardo's followers in Congress might thwart him. Congress was promptly sent home and a national assembly was convoked to

[1] See John E. Fagg, *Latin America: A General History*. New York, Macmillan Company, 1963.

draw up a new Constitution. "Peru smilingly contemplates," its puppet presiding officer droned, "the ideal that dawns upon her after a century of errors and sadness." The first article of the old charter to go was the one prohibiting a President from succeeding himself. A Bill of Rights was included but was never honored in practice.

Leguía was born at Lambayeque in 1863. Of an affluent family, he was educated in Valparaiso, Chile, where his father had been doing business. Enlisting in the Peruvian Army at the outbreak of the War of the Pacific, he had been wounded at Miraflores. He began building his first fortune as agent for an American life insurance company—an experience that probably accounts both for his administrative efficiency and for his lifelong partiality for American businessmen. He was a very small man, weighing less than a hundred pounds, quiet-spoken, and with searching cold eyes. His audacity was likened to that of a gamecock. His admirers compared him variously to Napoleon, Mussolini, and Franklin D. Roosevelt. Like all Peruvian dictators, he posed as a protector of the Indians.

The hopes of the emerging middle class on which Leguía had ridden to power were realized only to the extent that many were able to profit by the ten years of prosperity that preceded the financial collapse of 1931. In respect to institutions and parties, the middle class found no outlet for its aspirations. Freedom of expression was not tolerated. Even economically the middle class had to be satisfied with the crumbs from the tables of the oligarchs. Were it not that these well-spread tables were dwarfed by those set up for favored foreign interests, Leguía's dictatorship might have lasted longer than it did.

The vast public-works program that kept Leguía afloat was financed in part by foreign loans and in part by investments of foreign capital. Peru's foreign debt increased in ten years from $10,000,000 to $110,000,000. Land grants of tens of thousands of acres went to the Leguía family in Loreto Province. It was revealed later by an investigation in the United States Senate that Juan Leguía, the President's son, had received a $415,000 "commission" for placing one Peruvian loan of $100,000,000 with the Seligman banking house in New York. W. R. Grace & Co., Cerro de Pasco Copper, the Vanadium Corporation, and other American businesses received handsome concessions. Standard Oil of New Jersey replaced a British company that had been working the vast petroleum field at Talara on the north coast—an imperialist switch that plagues Peruvian politics to this day. The resewering of Lima and the paving of its principal streets, together with the construction of sanitation facilities for thirty-one other cities, was undertaken by the Foundation Company of New York. An American naval captain, Frank B. Freyer, was brought in to reorganize the sea forces and was made chief of staff. American educational experts were invited to Peru. One of them, H. Edwin Bard, was made Director General of Instruction. Another, Albert Giesecke, became Mayor of Cuzco. Huge irrigation works were built under the supervision of an American engineer, C. W. Sutton. Highways and railroads proliferated under the same auspices.

Much was accomplished in all these fields, and Leguía even built himself an ornate marble palace where Pizarro's home had stood, but the humiliating sense that foreigners were once again taking over Peru combined with other circumstances to bring about the dictator's fall. The world deflation in the mining and agricultural markets not only weakened Leguía's support among the oligarchy; it brought with it fear among the landowners that, unless a more flexible climate should prevail, unrest might trigger a genuine revolt of the masses.

The first student uprising had taken place at Cuzco in 1909. In Trujillo a pro-Indian movement strongly influenced by Mexico's proletarian revolution of 1910 had been born. On May 23, 1923, Victor Raúl Haya de la Torre, one of these Trujillo students, had led a huge student-labor demonstration at the University of San Marcos in Lima against Leguía's attempt to ingratiate himself with the Church by "dedicating" the country to the Sacred Heart of Jesus. Two demonstrators had died in the street fighting that ensued, Haya and the other leaders had been driven into exile, and the university was closed for three years. Nationalists, and even the military, had cooled to Leguía when he—who had criticized Pardo in 1919 for "failure to recover our lost provinces"—settled the Tacna-Arica question with Chile by conceding Arica to the latter forever.

On August 22, 1930, the revolt came. It erupted, as usual, in Arequipa, and with some semblance of spontaneity. It quickly became a praetorian affair, however, when the army, anxious to head off more dangerous, popular sponsorship, deposed Leguía in the capital and imprisoned him on San Lorenzo Island. The immediate beneficiary of the change was Col. Luis Sánchez Cerro, a mestizo who merely substituted a military despotism for the civilian one. The following year Sánchez Cerro had himself declared President in a rigged election (117,711 votes to 85,546) over Haya de la Torre. The real winner, and destined to be the dominant political figure in Peru for the next three decades, was Haya, the founder and leader of the popular movement known as APRA.

Haya de la Torre and APRA

The APRA (Alianza Popular Revolucionaria Americana) was a cellular movement, pan–Latin American and Indianist, founded by Haya in Mexico in 1924. Its transformation into a political party, the Partido Aprista Peruano, did not come until the political campaign of 1931, when Haya decided to run for the presidency against Sánchez Cerro. Down the years, movement and party have undergone as many changes as their colorful leader.

In the beginning APRA made common cause with the international Communist movement. However, the fact that it was spawned while Haya was serving as secretary to José Vasconcelos, then Mexican Minister of Education, a militant Catholic who was soon to be communism's bitterest foe, may have germinated seeds of independent thinking in its youthful founder's mind. The following year, on a trip to Russia, where Haya met the principal Soviet ideologists and was dismayed by their ignorance of Latin America, he became convinced that Marxism could not be exported without revisions. At the World Anti-Imperialist Congress in Brussels in 1927, the break became definitive. "For Communism," Haya wrote, "there could not exist another party of the Left." But during four years in Germany Haya had continued to think mainly in terms of the class struggle, and his references to democracy were not friendly. Returning to Mexico in 1928, he summed up APRA'S program as: (1) action against imperialism; (2) for the political unity of Latin America; (3) for the nationalization of land and industry; (4) for the internationalization of the Panama Canal; and (5) for solidarity with all oppressed peoples and classes of the world.[2]

Nothing the Communists could take exception to there, except perhaps the pluralistic tone of Point 5. Haya indeed was beginning to think now in terms of a broad-based party uniting workers, peasants, *and the middle classes*. In fact it is the middle class, as time goes on, that assumes the dominant role in the revolution Haya has in mind. Although the state must prevent abuse of its natural resources by foreign capital, it should welcome loans and technical

[2] Quoted in Robert J. Alexander, *Prophets of the Revolution* (New York, Macmillan Company, 1962), which contains the best summary in English of Haya's thinking.

assistance from abroad when properly controlled. Political democracy, or "functional democracy," as Haya calls it, is seen to be essential if the state is not to simply pass from a dictatorship of the Right to one of the Left. Cooperatives, developed along Inca lines, are to be the instruments of the Indians' regeneration. Regional and international "common markets" will ensure that the separate Latin American nations share their divided resources and are enabled to compete with the Colossus of the North.

During World War II APRA's program, but not its philosophy, was modified to support the war against German and Japanese totalitarianism.[3] In the postwar period the movement's support of Manuel Prado, and more recently its alliance with its old adversary, ex-dictator Manuel Odría, in opposition to President Belaúnde, have placed APRA considerably to the Right of Center in the political spectrum.

The strength and weakness of Aprismo, in all its ups and downs, can be equated absolutely with the personality of its leader. Mercurial, intellectually curious and speculative, eccentric, selfless and yet somehow self-centered, dedicated but unstable, a Bohemian who has always preferred good talk and travel to the drudgery of administration and power, Haya de la Torre has made a private success out of party failure, a romance out of defeat. At seventy he is as charismatic, as godlike in the eyes of his followers, and as unpredictable as he always was.

Phase I: APRA Goes Underground

Haya's fame as a radical theoretician and agitator antedated by many years his founding of the most influential political movement in Latin America's history. He was born in Trujillo in 1895 of an aristocratic family whose name indicates descent from Juan de la Torre, one of Pizarro's thirteen indomitable "men of Gallo." The un-Spanish cast of his features Haya was pleased to compare to a hook-nosed Chimu profile in the nearby ruins of Chan Chan. As a youthful member of the Indianist cultural movement in Trujillo be-

[3] In an interview with Haya and an article by him, published in the March and November 1941 issues of the magazine *Common Sense*, edited by the author of this book, Haya expressed the view that APRA would support the war against the Axis powers even if it became necessary to invite North American forces to Peru to repel invasion. But he added that the Good Neighbor Policy of Franklin D. Roosevelt must be extended to include support for democratic governments in Latin America and implacable hostility toward dictatorships. "It must be understood that the defense of democracy is not merely a *military defense* but a *civil and moral defense* of the liberties it proclaims."

fore World War I, Haya's friends included José Eulógio Garrido, founder of the city's archaeological museum, and César Vallejo, destined to be Peru's greatest poet. At the University of San Marcos in Lima Haya became president of the student federation, supported a successful general strike for the eight-hour day, assisted in establishing Peru's first national labor union, organized the first national student congress, signed the first inter-American student pact. More than any other man Haya was responsible for substituting in the universities of Latin America control by faculty and students for control by Church and state—a measure that seemed progressive and democratic at the time, but which Haya lived to regret when the "autonomous" campuses became hotbeds of communism following World War II.

Haya's expulsion from Peru following the bloody anti-Leguía demonstration of May 23, 1923, has already been mentioned. When he returned to Peru eight years later to run for the presidency against the despotic Sánchez Cerro, Haya found himself the idol of labor and the Indian peasants as well as of the students. But there ensued the first of that series of repressions of APRA that drove the movement underground, turned it toward terrorism, and gives it its defensive, conspiratorial complexion to this day.

No sooner had the victorious Haya been counted out in the 1932 election than he and the principal Apristas were seized and brought to trial. The leadership in Trujillo staged an insurrection. Twenty-six soldiers were found shot in their barracks. Not only did Sánchez Cerro crush the revolt. He gave orders that five thousand Apristas were to be rounded up in the provincial capital and set to digging trenches. When the trenches were dug, the prisoners were toppled into them by machine-gun fire. Relations between APRA and the Army were poisoned permanently.

When the ruthless Sánchez Cerro was assassinated on April 30, 1933, it was charged that an Aprista had killed him. But Gen. Óscar Benavides, who succeeded Sánchez Cerro in the presidency, made a truce with APRA, restored its congressmen to their positions, released Haya from jail—only to reverse himself and instigate another manhunt a few months later.

This time Haya managed to evade the police and remained in hiding for a decade. From his various hideaways he must have watched with grim amusement the tragicomedy of betrayals and unholy alliances with which Benavides and his successor, the millionaire banker Manuel Prado, managed to evade the popular clamor for Aprista rule. In 1936, when the tiny Social Democratic Party

7

was permitted to run a presidential candidate of its own, Haya sent out word that Apristas were to vote for him. He was winning by a landslide when Benavides seized the ballot boxes and announced in panic that he himself would remain in office another three years. To break the power of APRA in the trade unions, Sánchez Cerro, Benavides, and even Prado thought nothing of accepting the support of the Communists—a piece of brazen cynicism on the part of the latter that foreshadowed the infamous Nazi-Soviet Pact that triggered World War II, and that may account for the failure of the Communist *guerrilleras* in 1965 to receive an iota of popular support.

Phase II: APRA Veers to the Right

Either out of fear that the Communists might now come to dominate the labor and peasant masses in Peru, or in the mistaken belief that the underground leadership of APRA had lost touch with its following, President Prado and his mentor, ex-President Benavides, came to an agreement in 1945: the outlawed party would be permitted to participate in the elections that year (though not under its own name), and Haya would be allowed to come out of hiding. It was too late for APRA to name a presidential candidate of its own, but it ran a full slate for the Senate and Chamber of Deputies, and it threw its support behind José Bustamente Rivero, a moderate pledged to end all repressive laws. Bustamente won easily, and kept his word. APRA controlled the new Congress.

Haya de la Torre was now the unacknowledged ruler of Peru. It was inevitable that his views, and those of APRA, which had by now taken control of the labor movement away from the Communists, would clash with those of the President, the Army, and the oligarchy. The showdown came in October of 1948. An APRA-led naval mutiny in Callao Harbor took place. Haya disowned it, but President Bustamente was pressured into outlawing APRA again. This time the Army acted to prevent another accommodation with its bitter foe. The garrison in Arequipa revolted, and the Minister of Defense, Gen. Manuel Odría, took the occasion to oust the liberal President Bustamente. After a prolonged manhunt, the ailing Haya was obliged to take refuge in the Colombian Embassy.

For six years the celebrated refugee remained prisoner in the very center of the country that clamored for his leadership. It was the most bizarre chapter in a lifetime spent in flights from persecution. The embassy was surrounded by slit trenches and gun positions. All approaches were roadblocked. Searchlights played on the isolated white building by night. The prisoner was unable to walk in the garden or appear at a window lest he be shot from the surrounding rooftops. Yet he was interviewed by the world press, received delegations, issued pronouncements, and kept in close touch with his clandestine movement. Colombia and Peru accused each other of improper conduct, but the Colombian Ambassador showed admirable fortitude in standing up for the right of asylum—at that time the longest invocation of it on record. The case was taken to the International Court of Justice in The Hague, which issued a typical judgment satisfying no one. Finally, in 1954, Haya was permitted to go into exile once more.

When the APRA leader returned to Peru in 1956 for another messianic welcome, the movement's stance had drastically changed. Ramiro Priale, the wily party organizer, had had to make a choice in the three-cornered presidential race now underway between Odría's stand-in, Hernando Lavalle, former President Manuel Prado, and a young newcomer, the liberal architect Fernando Belaúnde Terry. Belaúnde as Deputy had worked closely with the Apristas, but Priale, fearing that APRA would lose its traditional student-labor following to the magnetic Belaúnde, backed Prado, after extracting a promise that the Aprista Party would be promptly legalized.[4] Prado won easily, and kept his promise—which was believed to ensure the presidency for Haya in 1962. But APRA's romantic-radical image was tarnished.

Haya himself had prefigured the shift to the Right when calling the shots under Bustamente: he had disenchanted his followers by advocating that Peru compensate American investors for the worthless bonds floated in the Leguía period, and he had advocated a strict press censorship—presumably to cover up APRA's failure to make any headway with its program of land reform. Now, by making a deal with the millionaire conservative chief executive in return for mere party legality, Priale was ensuring precisely what he had intended to avoid. In the decade ahead, APRA would retain its hold only over the now stodgy labor movement it had sired in the days of its militancy and over government workers in the middle and lower echelons. A growing percentage of the youth, and to a large

[4] Many Apristas contend that Belaúnde refused to guarantee APRA's legality, if elected, while Prado did. This, they say, fits in with his alleged refusal to make an agreement with APRA in 1962, at which time, it is said, he was offered the support necessary for election in the Congress if he would include Apristas in his Cabinet.

extent the unorganized Indian and urban masses, would throw their support to Belaúnde's more hungry Acción Popular.

In the decade 1956–66, as APRA completed its drift to conservatism by finally making an alliance with Odría himself, Haya's personality seemed unchanged. His enemies went on insinuating that he got an erotic charge out of public speaking, and instead of accusing him of being a Communist or a Fascist as in the past, they now ridiculed him as a *causeur,* a dilettante, a traveling narcissist in love with his own waywardness. The fact was that Haya's buoyant idealism had not left him. He remained as strongly committed to his program of Indian regeneration, cooperative land reform, and Latin American unity as he ever had been. But in politics Haya's naïveté left him at the mercy of less principled men. His intellectual's indifference to administrative detail separated him from the day-to-day maneuvers that set the party adrift in a sea of intrigue, first alienating the middle classes by terrorism and threats of expropriation and finally losing the support of the dispossessed by the tactical compromises that aligned APRA with the very forces of reaction it had been born to destroy.

The Dictatorship of General Odría

It is time to return now to the years between 1948 and 1956, when Manuel Odría was giving Peru a reasonable facsimile of the order, prosperity, economic development, and authoritarian rule it had experienced under Leguía. Unlike Leguía, Odría was a military man who made no attempt to pose as a man of the people or a democrat, but he was quite Leguía's equal in constructive energy and shrewdness. Like Leguía, he ruled from a power base that included only the armed forces and the oligarchy, but changes in the outside world, particularly in neighboring Bolivia, tended to make Odría wary of alienating the common people by naked repression, and more anxious to channel Peru's resources into public works that would indirectly benefit them.

A social revolution was being carried out at this time in La Paz by Victor Paz Estenssoro—with United States acquiescence. Paz in 1951 had taken over the tin mines, enfranchised and armed the illiterate peasants, and divided up many of the big haciendas among three quarters of a million landless Indian families. This Bolivian phenomenon was leading the moneyed classes in Lima to think in terms of self-preserving reforms. Odría's reforms were mild enough.

But he did abolish exchange controls, and the resulting flow of foreign investment enabled Peru to diversify exports and thus escape the inflation afflicting most other South American countries. Foreign capital and technology were invited to Peru, and came. An American mission provided financial guidance. The bureaucracy was pared down and trained in modern methods of efficiency. The Korean War resulted in a great increase in prices for Peru's products, and Odría's budget expanded in accordance with the opportunity. During the dictatorship—and during Prado's second term (1956–62) which was a less despotic but more bumbling extension of the same system—road building and irrigation projects expanded the amazingly small part of Peru devoted to agriculture. New industries sprang up along the coast, and one of them, fish meal, alone turned recession back into boom when the prices of sugar, cotton, and copper fell on the world market after the conclusion of the Korean War.

Nothing was done to change the status of the Indians. At the close of the sixteenth century they had constituted over 90 percent of the population. Under the colony their numbers diminished somewhat; it had been relatively easy to "pass over" into the mestizo ranks. But following independence the Indian community, more isolated than ever, once again began to outstrip in growth the mestizos and whites. In the twentieth century, with industrialization demanding a reservoir of cheap labor and highlanders beginning to migrate in large numbers into the coastal region, the trend has reversed itself again. By 1940, according to Kubler, only 42 percent of Peru's population could be classified as Indian, and this bloc was concentrated very largely in the central highlands between Huánuco and Lake Titicaca. Odría, responding to the new oligarchic creed that economic development carried far enough must bring prosperity to everybody, began to undertake a nationwide campaign against illiteracy. For the first time the Indian communities got schools, though the instruction provided was primitive, and there was seldom an opportunity for the poverty-stricken Indian to take advantage of his Spanish or other tokens of the patrón's culture.

One educational innovation, however, did have revolutionary implications. In 1952 Cornell University, in collaboration with the Instituto Indigenista Peruano, was permitted to sublet for five years a hacienda called Vicos, a Quechua-speaking community of two thousand inhabitants in the Callejón de Huaylas. The idea was to see whether a "backward" community would take to the most modern agricultural techniques and in time manage its own economy. Not only did agriculture prosper in the project as never before in Peru; when the Americans withdrew and the government was induced to let the Indians fend for themselves on a collective basis, *the level of output on the community lands rose by 600 percent*. "Once the Vicosinos assumed direct control of the hacienda, a new perspective on the future, a new lease on life was possible. They now had a stake in their own destiny." [5] The people, in other words, had been taught how to help themselves. The hacendados, of course, saw to it that their government in Lima did not extend this happy experiment to other communities, but the success of Vicos was to affect strongly the drive for cooperatives and self-help projects among the Indians under Belaúnde in the sixties.

One other aspect of the Odría-Prado period deserves mention. That face of Peru which the visitor sees changed dramatically: Lima, with over a million inhabitants now, became a modern metropolis. There were skyscrapers, luxury hotels, bathing beaches, shopping centers, movie theaters, airports—and traffic problems. It became possible to fly throughout Peru. The provincial cities themselves, and little by little the outlying districts as far as the jungle borders, in turn were getting the message. Illustrated magazines, the radio, the cinema were unfolding a vision of well-dressed and healthy people with jobs and cars, living in cities. The mass migration out of the cold, disease-ridden, infertile highlands into the warm, flourishing river valleys began. The reality—city slums and unemployment—was never pictured in the technicolored propaganda. Very soon Lima, and to a slightly lesser degree Trujillo, Piura, Chimbote, Arequipa, and even jungle-bound Iquitos were ringed with shantytowns thrown together out of packing crates and straw mats. Bad as it was, life *was* better, or seemed to be; the migrants were there to stay. And Odría, yielding to the pressure, permitted them to squat (rent free generally) and to keep coming. Peru had taken on another major problem: the *barriadas*.

In the last years of his dictatorship Odría lost the support of the oligarchy. Businessmen with ideas of their own were thrown into jail with as little compunction as Apristas. No doubt the pressure building up in the barriadas was held against the General too. President Prado permitted more freedom of expression, and let APRA return to the scene. But there was a sudden slump in the world market, the United States imposed quota restrictions on the importation of lead and zinc, a drought in the south forced Peru to import food

[5] Alan Holmberg, Director of the Peru-Cornell Project, as quoted in David A. Robinson's *Peru in Four Dimensions*. Lima, American Studies Press, 1964.

in large quantities for the first time, prices began to rise, and the sol depreciated.[6] In 1959 Prado gave special powers to Pedro Beltrán, the wealthy owner of *La Prensa* and an economist, and Beltrán did manage to stabilize the sol, give Peru a favorable balance of payments, and stimulate foreign investments; but very little of this prosperity at the top filtered down to the masses. And every effort to supplement "austerity" with cheap housing, minimal land reform, or colonization of the montaña bogged down in an obstructionist Congress. The stage was set for another bang-up Peruvian election.

There were seven presidential candidates in June of 1962, but only three of them were in the running. The first official count gave Haya 558,000 votes, Belaúnde 543,000, and Odría 481,400. The other four candidates, one of whom was Hector Cornéjo Chavez, leader of the vociferous Christian Democrat movement, polled less than 50,000 each. Predictably, Haya was once again disqualified, this time on the constitutional grounds that Congress must decide the outcome if no party should receive 33⅓ percent of the total vote, and on June 18 the Army sent its tanks crashing through the wrought-iron gates of the Presidential Palace. Prado was seized, and a military junta announced that new elections would be held the following June. In Washington President John F. Kennedy denounced the coup, broke diplomatic relations, suspended military and economic aid. But relations were resumed when the junta pledged itself to maintain freedom of the press and civil liberties and to respect the winner of the coming year's election—whoever might win.

In the elections of June 1963 Belaúnde, now supported by the Christian Democrats, polled 708,900 votes to Haya's 623,500 and Odría's 463,000. Since the coalition of Acción Popular and the Christian Democrats did not win a majority in either the Senate or the Chamber of Deputies, and since the Apristas and Odriístas (now startlingly allied) did, the new President was assured of frustration even before he took office.

The Presidency of Fernando Belaúnde Terry

The great-grandson of President Diez Canseco (*see* pp. 64–65) and nephew of Victor Andrés Belaúnde, a conservative Catholic libertarian who had been jailed and ousted from Peru by Leguía and in Paris had published an impassioned plea for Andean confederation as the best means of resisting foreign domination, Fernando Belaúnde

[6] In 1966 the sol was worth approximately four (U.S.) cents.

Terry was well prepared by birth and upbringing for the role he was destined to assume. A social reformer in Peru who is not at once an aristocrat and a Catholic is impossibly handicapped. To come from an Arequipa family is to have the spirit of revolt in one's blood. To be brought up in exile sharpens the critical temper as well as one's patriotism. A childhood friend remembers the tiny room in Paris which the boy Fernando decked with flags and called "The Real Peruvian Consulate." Evidently the despotic style of the ruler in Lima was abhorrent to the little patriot.

Born in Lima on October 7, 1912, Belaúnde was eighteen when his father moved from Paris to Miami on a teaching assignment, and enrolled him in the university's architectural school. In 1933, with Leguía gone, the father accepted a diplomatic post in Mexico and the son enrolled at the University of Texas. Returning to Peru after graduation, the young man made a name for himself as a regional planner and housing expert, and in 1950 he was appointed Dean of the School of Architecture at the Escuela Nacional de Ingenieros. Elected to the Chamber of Deputies in 1945, he waged a spirited fight for low-cost urban housing, designing some of the pioneer projects in Peru himself. After travels abroad during the first years of the Odría dictatorship, he returned to launch himself as an independent candidate for the 1956 election.

It was in the next three years that the handsome young idealist won a name for himself almost comparable to Haya's—"romantic" in the eyes of his friends, "demagogic" as seen by his foes. When Odría attempted to disqualify his candidacy in 1956, he forced the dictator to back down by leading a mob of a thousand through tear gas to the National Palace. Defeated in the election, he now organized his own party, the Acción Popular. By making an unprecedented election tour of all the provinces and attempting through his oratory to shake the Indians out of their coca-chewing lethargy, he came close to winning. He fought an inconclusive duel with sabers on a Lima rooftop against a political opponent who had called him a liar. When Prado clapped him in jail for several days for holding a rally in defiance of a presidential ban, he enhanced his reputation for adventurousness by trying to escape Frontón Island by swimming. In Arequipa, in the aftermath of the tank-crushed 1962 election, he led his followers in a noisy street demonstration. But the following year, when elected President in the second contest with Haya and Odría, Belaúnde at once addressed himself seriously to the problems plaguing Peru.

The Program of Acción Popular

Belaúnde the romantic nationalist, and Belaúnde the visionary reformer, coexist in the glowing pages of *Peru's Own Conquest.*[7] It is a vision both mystic and practical, a journey through Peru that will strike some readers as sentimental and others as transcendental. The floating slums of Iquitos, whose inhabitants sometimes eat the rats that live on the sewage, are described as "a community already incorporated into civilization, vibrant with Peruvianism . . . illuminated more by the diaphanous and everlasting light of faith than by the burning tropical sun." The brutal Conquest is described as if it were an episode in chivalry. Belaúnde can seriously speak of "the people's intuition, that profound sense possessed by multitudes." Yet in the context of his love affair with Peru and his impassioned desire to see it save itself by its own spiritual resources, everything is of a piece. The canals of Belén *are* ingenious, and beautiful—from a distance. Peru can't do without willpower and daring, the conquistadores' only redeeming characteristics. Belaúnde will say anything to reawaken the Incaic collective responsibility. "Modern Peru," he says more cogently, "is overshadowed by the irrefutable superiority of the ancients in the battle to win land from the desert." In a spirit that Frank Lloyd Wright would have applauded, he rhapsodizes over the builders of the great aqueducts and andenes—"works of art which rise from a skillful marriage of structure with the earth . . . dynamic forms freed from their elemental geometry. . . . The builder does not mistreat the topography, but rather seems to caress it." And then he tells how he crossed the Andes on horseback and by foot—"not to lose the sense of human perspective." One is moved by this identification with the land, and even more by the man's humanity. There is an unforgettable story of a man on a jungle riverboat who had lost both hands while working on the Pucallpa highway; one shares Belaúnde's anger when he speaks of the "glacial indifference" of governments that fail to indemnify such victims—and when he says that one of his first acts after becoming President was to see that this fellow human being received a pension, it seems credible.

As he journeys from desert to highlands, to the Amazon and back, Belaúnde's social philosophy reveals itself. He is looking for a system "combining the advantages of capitalism and socialism without

[7] By Fernando Belaúnde Terry. With an Introduction by D. A. Robinson. Lima, American Studies Press, 1965.

the faults both systems bring: speculation on the one hand and destruction of private initiative on the other. . . . Banks should not continue being institutions that 'lend the poor man's money to the wealthy.' " What he calls Mestisaje, a blending of the Spanish and Indian virtues, is offered as the key to Peru's future. But to achieve it the Indian must recapture his pre-Columbian capacity to work constructively in collective harmony. The agency known as Cooperación Popular will give the mountain man the tools, the knowledge, and perhaps the pride to help himself. The Agrarian Reform Law will provide the landless Indian with "a parcel of land capable of supporting him." And the third and most visionary component of the Belaúnde program, a Marginal Highway along the fertile and unoccupied eastern slope of the Andes, will provide not only the means of colonizing the millions of dispossessed who have drifted into the barriadas, but a physical linkage to the economic common market so badly needed by all the republics stretching along the cordillera from Venezuela to the Argentine.

Under Fire from Right and Left

None of these three programs was exactly new. A hundred years earlier, as we have seen, Manuel Pardo projected the need to develop the eastern slopes of the Andes. In the second Prado administration, Pedro Beltrán had formed a cabinet with the express purpose of colonizing the montaña and limiting the size of haciendas to 250 acres on the coast and 1,000 in the highlands and jungle, but his program had bogged down in the Congress. Agrarian land reform and Indian cooperatives along Incaic lines had always been the foundation of Haya's thinking. But never before had a President taken power pledged to such a program, or brought to the office such wide-ranging familiarity with the country, such eloquence, and such energy.

If these gifts, combined with selflessness and immense personal popularity had been enough, Belaúnde's program would have been well on its way to fulfillment by 1966. Unfortunately for Peru, many circumstances conspired to make progress slow. Apristas and Odriístas, however different their motives, used their combined majority in the Congress to block or dilute many important pieces of legislation. As an administrator, the President proved to be less decisive and aggressive than had been hoped. The Right accused him of using Cooperación Popular to build a political machine in the highlands. His supporters on the Left (the Christian Democrats especially) charged that he was dragging his feet. In the crossfire of a virulent campaign to expropriate the International Petroleum Company the President was caught in the middle, hesitating to take a position that would offend either side.[8] Similarly, when several bands of Castro-backed guerrilleros in the mountains back of Huancayo and Cuzco incited Indians to seize remote haciendas and killed provincial police seeking to restrain them, Belaúnde, again under pressure from the Christian Democrats and the Communist-led university students, lightly brushed aside the rebels as "cattle rustlers"—only to have to eat his words.

The day following the presidential statement seven rural policemen were ambushed and their bodies were brought to the capital. The Army and the congressional opposition demanded action. Belaúnde suspended constitutional guarantees for thirty days. A military court was established with powers to sentence any guerrilla to death. Troops and artillery were flown into the trouble spots. The President issued a statement charging that Moscow and Peking as well as Havana were supplying the rebels. And by September of 1965, after a campaign lasting less than four months, the guerrilleros were eliminated. Had they received from the Indians even a quarter of the support they were getting from the university students, this would not have been possible. The fact was that the three-part Belaúnde program was generating unprecedented hope through the highlands.

Was that hope justified? As much as a generation might have to pass before a conclusive answer can be made. After a bad start Cooperación Popular, the Peruvian version of the American Peace Corps, was working wonders in many depressed areas.[9] The actual roads, schools, and irrigation ditches built might not add up to much physically, but the psychological effect of the effort on the Indian, and his astonishment to see white men from the cities working *with their hands* in his behalf, constituted a revolution in itself. Moreover, by prevailing on students to spend their vacations assisting the project, Belaúnde was providing both a practical answer to the Marxist dogma and an outlet for frustrated idealism.

[8] The campaign was launched by the Miró Quesada family, owners of the pro-government newspaper *El Comercio,* whose oil interests had been damaged when Leguía gave the former British concession at Talara to Standard Oil. The Communists and Christian Democrats fanned the anti-American campaign in their own interests.

[9] The Peace Corps had more than five hundred young men and women in Peru in 1966, living with the Indians and in the barriadas, countering effectively the Communists' anti-American propaganda—by their deeds.

Right-wing critics of the various Agrarian Reform laws pointed out that in almost every instance of their application, agricultural production declined. The criticism was true but irrelevant. It would take a generation for Indians to operate their new holdings efficiently. If many promptly sold their sheep or llamas for a quick profit, it was because they were destitute or lacked the education to provide for the future. If such programs had been provided with sufficient funds to include fertilizers, machinery, and training in the building of cooperatives, the initial results would have looked more promising. The moderate version of President Belaúnde's Agrarian Reform Law which the Peruvian Congress finally passed provided for both an extension of communal holdings and small individual proprietors. While the government has moved slowly in administering this law, it has given the peasants hope and cut the ground out from under the guerrillas.

The Marginal Highway was being ridiculed by Haya, who said, "Everyone knows that it makes no sense to transport Ecuadorean bananas to Bolivia's banana plantations—everyone except Belaúnde." [10] But here again, in the long view, the project did make sense. The major emphasis in any case was on building all-weather access roads from the coast to the montaña, roads that would have to precede any serious effort to "colonize" the rich eastern slopes of the Andes. And in this agonizingly slow conquest of the most difficult terrain in the Americas, Belaúnde was receiving much help from American engineering firms and the AID (Agency for International Development) missions.

The Population Explosion

One problem that was not being tackled realistically, and that in the end might undo the solutions to all the others, was the increase in population. Almost all of Belaúnde's impressive housing program was devoted to apartments for the middle and upper middle classes. The theory was that as the middle class moved out of its deteriorating dwellings, the slum dwellers would move up a notch, and in turn be supplanted by those in the improvised barriadas. Actually the number of people living in the old slums, many of them adjacent to garbage dumps and open sewers, and in the barriadas increased. In Lima, the population of a million that existed in the fifties had doubled. At least 50 percent of these two millions were living in

[10] From an interview with Haya de la Torre in the author's article, "Peruvian Politics Stalls Belaúnde's Reforms," in *The Reporter*, July 14, 1966.

dwellings unfit for animals. From 1950 to 1958, when the population of Peru was increasing by 19.5 percent, there was a 13 percent drop in food production. A decade later the per-capita income of Peruvians ($365) was rising, but not nearly fast enough; more than half the population, the sierra Indians, was producing only 7 percent of the gross national product; and the enormous new potential of fish meal, instead of going to human consumption, was being exported, at enormous profit, to feed European pigs and poultry. The population of Peru at present rates is increasing annually by 250,000 and is doubling every twenty years. For the time being, the barriada dweller is thinking as a small proprietor, content to scrounge for odd jobs, to improve his miserable home with admirable ingenuity and, when he can, buy a television set and sell viewing privileges to his less enterprising neighbors. But how long can this last if the population keeps growing? President Belaúnde, a good Catholic, thought that if Peru's resources were fully developed to feed its people, big families would be a blessing as in times past. One of his friends and advisers was less optimistic:

> All the proposed programs for industrialization and increased agricultural productivity, all the processes necessary to enable Peru to create a better life for all the inhabitants and play a significant role in the world community —can all these plans and aspirations be realistically attained if the population growth remains unchecked? The answer is no. . . . Some time sooner or later Peru must decide whether it is to have an unlimited population of starving people. . . . No Christian can successfully argue on the basis of natural law, or any other grounds, that it is just and right to bring children into the world to face sure poverty, misery, starvation, disease, and a high probability of death before reaching five years of age.[11]

Surely it would be a sorry quirk of history if the most capable President Peru has ever had—and the one most genuinely ambitious for his country—should in the end be thwarted by a force that is still controllable, his plans overrun by the march of the yet unborn.

[11] David A. Robinson, *op. cit.*

Part II
ILLUSTRATIONS

Plate 1. A stone relief figure from Chavín de Huantar, c. 850–300 B.C.

Plate 2. A stone monolithic sculpture from an unidentified culture in Callejón de Huaylas. (*Museum, Huarás*).

Abraham Guillen

Plate 3. A figure carved in relief from the same culture as that shown above. (*Museum, Huarás*).

Plate 4. Drawing from the Sun Gate at Tiahuanaco, Bolivia, showing the Cat God whose cult swept over Peru about 1000 A.D.

Plate 5. An early pre-Columbian embroidered mantle from Paracas necropolis. (*National Archaeological Museum, Lima*).

Martin Chambi

Plate 6. Two types of
terracing (andenes) invented
by Mochica engineers and
adapted (as shown here) by the
Incas at Pisac.

Plate 7. *Left,* **black and white ceramic Moon Goddess and** *right,* **painted jug with pelican handle and geometric design. Both from late pre-Columbian Chancay culture.**

Plate 8. Realistic portrait of a man in painted ceramic, Mochica culture, c. 400–1000 A.D. (*National Archaeological Museum, Lima.*)

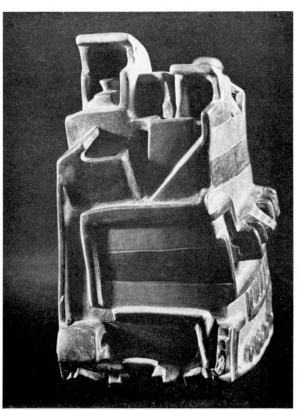

Plate 9. A ceramic from Moche showing the ingenious architecture of houses with vents to pick up sea breezes for cooling their interiors.

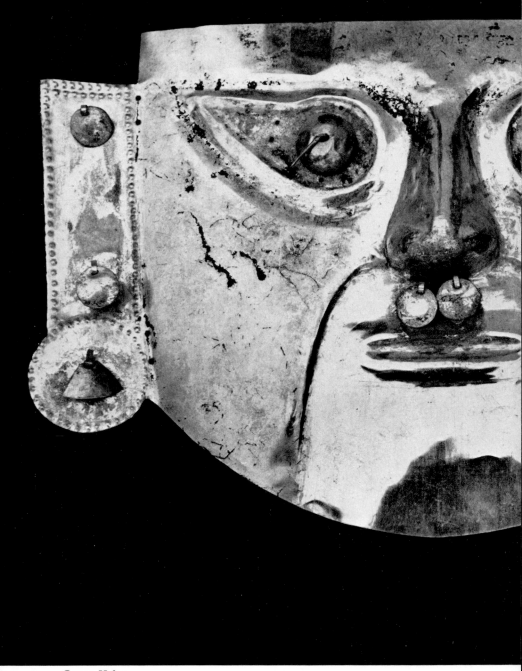

Plate 10. A Chimu funerary mask of gold from the *Miguel Mujica Gallo Collection.*

Plate 11. A painted wooden ceremonial vase of the late-Inca period.

Abraham Guillen

Plate 14. Machu Picchu. Ruins of the late-Inca fortress city showing Huayna Picchu looming over Urubamba gorge in the background.

Victor Chambi

Martin Chambi

Plate 15. A fiesta at the foot of Mount Ausangate, near Cuzco. It re-enacts the resistance of the Indians to the Conquest.

Alfred M. Bingham

Plate 16. Hiram Bingham, discoverer of Machu Picchu.

Plate 17. Equestrian statue of Conqueror Francisco Pizarro.

Author

Plate 18. Megalithic angled redoubts of Sacsahuamán Fortress, overlooking Cuzco, which failed to stop the Spaniards.

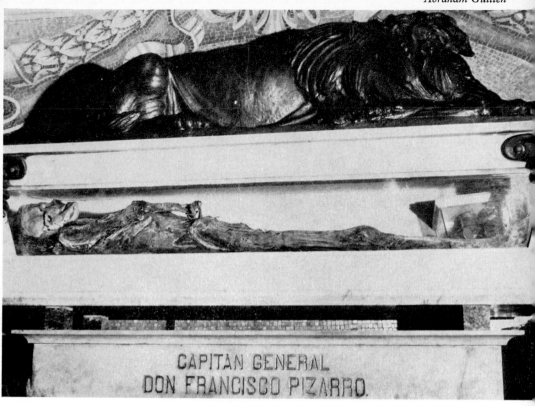

CAPITAN GENERAL
DON FRANCISCO PIZARRO.

Plate 19. The mummified remains of Pizarro in the Cathedral at Lima.

Plate 20. A painting of a typical Viceroy of Peru in the mid-eighteenth century. (*National Historical Museum, Lima.*)

Abraham Guillen

**Plate 21. The Jesuit parish church at Cayma, outside of Arequipa.
White volcanic stone is typical of this region.**

**Plate 22. The baroque façade of La Compañí
a Jesuit Church in Arequipa, dated 169**

Martin Cham

Plate 23. The main square at Arequipa, showing the Cathedral (a modern restoration) and snow-capped Mount Misti.

Author

Plate 24. A portrait of Simón Bolívar, painted from life in Lima by José Gil de Castro. (*National Historical Museum, Lima.*)

Abraham Guillen

117

Plate 25. José de San Martín, painted from life in Lima by José Gil de Castro. (*Military Circle, Lima.*)

Plate 27. The baro⋅ carved pulpi⋅ San Blas Chur⋅ Cuz⋅

Plate 26. Painting of Alfonso Ugarte, hero the War of the Pacifi (*National Historical Museum, Lima.*)

Plate 28. Carved and burnished gourds (matés) from Huancayo.

Plate 29. An Indian craftsman at Pucará with ceramic bulls and horses for which the town is famous. The figurines are in the last stages of modelling and later will be glazed.

Plate 30. Indians in traditional silver-bangled costumes worn in the Fiesta of San Pedro, near Huancayo.

Plate 32. Looking across the bay at fashionable Ancon.

Author

Plate 31. The façade of the Presidential Palace, Plaza de Armas, Lima.

Victor Chambi

Plate 33. Barriada dwellings in which half of Lima's population lives. It is built on mountains of refuse and flushed by the river Rímac.

Emil Willimetz

Plate 35. Shipibo decoration on the doors of a church, Lake Yarinacocha, Pucallpa.

Plate 34. Monumental statue of Francisco Bolognesi, hero of the Battle of Arica, Tacna.

Plate 36. President Fernando Belaúnde Terry.

George Holton

Emil Willimetz

Plate 37. Peruvian harps (cerpas) carried in procession by Indians in ponchos and knitted woollen hats near Pisac.

Plate 38. Balas, boats made from reeds, on Lake Titicaca. Shared by Peru and Bolivia, it is the highest lake in the world.

George Holton

Martin Chambi

Plate 39. Devil-dance mask worn during February fiestas, Puno.

Author

Plate 40. Yagua Indians demonstrating how to use blowguns on a tributary of the Amazon.

Plate 41. Belén, floating suburb of Iquitos on the Amazon.

George Holton

Plate 42. Children of Lima's Felicia Barriada waiting for hot school lunches. Peru faces many problems, especially health, education, unemployment and a mounting birth rate.

Part III

TRAVELOGUE

Tourists

NO country in the world has a greater variety of attractions to offer the visitor than Peru. Naturalists, art lovers, Alpinists, big-game hunters, archaeologists, spelunkers, desert-rats and jungle-rats, surf-boarders and trout fishermen, antiquarians and modernists, adventurers and invalids can find in one part or another of this most diversified of lands exactly what they are looking for—*if* they can get to it.

Where else but in Peru can one swim in hot mineral pools surrounded by plantations of pineapples and sugar cane under the shadow of peaks eternally covered with snow? Where else can one spend the morning savoring megalithic stonework and Baroque architecture and the afternoon fishing for thirty-pound lake trout or marketing among Indians dressed like medieval troubadours? Where but in Peru can one swim in the Pacific and then dig in the dunes on the beach for pre-Columbian sculpture or amulets of gold? ...Explore the Amazon and its uncharted tributaries, trade for blowguns and crowns of touçan feathers, *paiches'* tongues, and shrunken human heads....

Few of these things are easy to do, and the last may involve equipping a private safari; but the very fact that difficulties are involved and an adventurous spirit is needed is what makes them still possible.

Hotels and Communications

As of the season 1965–66 (the North American winter is Peru's summer, except in the mountains and jungle, where rainfalls bring the only seasonal changes), there were only three luxury hotels in Peru, all in the capital, and only four hotels with swimming pools—one in Tacna, of all places. Government-operated tourist hotels are to be found in all the principal cities of Peru, many of which offer nothing of interest to the tourist; these hotels are moderately expensive and clean, the food is good, and with few exceptions the management is inefficient and indifferent to a tourist's needs. There are pensions and cheap restaurants and bilingual guides in the same cities, and perhaps one day a nongovernment agency will be opened in Lima to direct tourists to the best of them.

Six means of travel within the country are available. There are the commercial airlines, Faucett and Lansa; and the Air Force–operated SATCO; the national railway system; buses; rented automobiles; and *colectivos* (taxis in which you can rent one seat). Rented automobiles are expensive, though gas is cheaper than in the United States; nor will the rental agencies permit their cars to operate beyond the coastal plain. Colectivos, however, travel everywhere—if somewhat dangerously. Buses travel everywhere except in jungle country where there are no roads, but neither time nor safety figure in this service, and the mountain roads are spine-chillingly hazardous. The railroads do run on time, but their snail-like penetration of the Andean barrier is available only from Lima through Huancayo to Huancavelica, and from Mollendo to Arequipa and Puno on Lake Titicaca, thence branching northwest to Cuzco and Machu Picchu.

That leaves the airways. Peruvian Airlines (Aerolineas Peruanas) offers the only nonstop flight from Miami to Lima, and its thoroughly reliable jets also connect the Peruvian capital with Los Angeles, Panama, Mexico City, and most of the South American capitals. Airways within Peru were pioneered by Elmer J. Faucett, an American World War I pilot who collected prize money for flying the first plane from Lima to Iquitos. Since 1929 Faucett passenger planes have negotiated the deserts, mountain peaks, and jungles of Peru with a remarkable record of safety and efficiency. Its DC-3's, DC-4's and DC-6's fly regularly and (weather permitting) on time from Lima to Cuzco (2 hours), Arequipa (2 hours, 10 minutes), Ayacucho (1 hour, 30 minutes), Trujillo (1 hour, 30 minutes), Piura (2 hours, 40 minutes), Cajamarca (2 hours, 50 minutes), Pucallpa (2 hours, 35 minutes), Iquitos (2 hours, 50 minutes), and to other less interesting places. Only Trujillo and Piura may be reached without flying over the high mountains. On the other flights, unpressurized cabins supply passengers with oxygen from tubes.

All flights from Lima originate at the new International Airport, an hour's drive from the center of the city.

Lima and Its Environs

Pizarro's City of Kings was founded by the Conquistador on January 6, 1535, Epiphany (Day of the Kings). The name Lima is a corruption of *Rímac*, a Quechua word meaning "He who speaks" and believed to refer to an Inca oracle at the site. The Rímac River waters the valley after descending from the Andes through the gorge up which Henry Meiggs's railroad labors on its way to La Oroya, Cerro de Pasco, and Huancayo. After reaching the city at the Plaza de Armas, the river veers westward, paralleling the waterfront, skirting the International Airport, and forming a kind of peninsula which terminates in the harbor of Callao. At the point of this peninsula is La Punta, the naval base and college which faces the islands of San Lorenzo and Frontón in the bay.

In the fan-shaped area between the river and the Pan American Highway stretching south lies the old city and most of the famous suburbs: Magdalena Nueva, San Isidro, Miraflores, Barranco, Chorrillos. At the apex of the fan is the Plaza de Armas, with the Government Palace and Cathedral, and below it the Plaza San Martín with the Hotel Bolívar and the airline offices. The narrow street called Jirón Unión connecting the two great squares is only six blocks long, but it is the shopping center of Lima. The city's main thoroughfare, however, begins the same distance southwest of the Plaza San Martín, where it is called Avenida Wilson, passing a park on which the American Embassy faces, and then continues southeasterly as the Avenida Arequipa, through the plush residential districts of San Isidro and Miraflores to the sea.

In San Isidro are to be found the Hotel Country Club, a famous luxury establishment with pools and tennis courts operated as a separate private concession; the Campo de Golf; the Anglo-American Clinic; the Criquet Club; and other institutions dear to the elite of three countries. Miraflores, with as many thousands of fine private dwellings, has a shopping plaza, gift shops, and supermarkets of its own. Farther south along the bay, Barranco and Chorrillos once contained the palatial homes of the oligarchs but never recovered from the devastation of the war with Chile. Here are to be found the zoo, the military school, and the first of many popular bathing beaches stretching south along the Pacific.

Lima, as with all of the coastal region, is free from extremes of heat and cold. The temperature averages 75° F. the year round. Its summer (December through May) is rainless and sunny; winter (June through November) rainless and foggy. The cold Peru Current sweeping up from the Antarctic keeps the climate from ever turning equatorial. It accounts as well for the desert, the moisture-laden atmosphere of the winter, and the abundance of fish. But the ocean, especially in summer, is pleasant to swim in, and the immense sand dunes up and down the coast are beautiful to look at.

Beaches and Ruins

Especially beautiful is the high coastal bluff running north of Lima past the harbor of Ancón to the valley of Chancay. The drive along the coastal highway at this point is spectacular—and a bit frightening. The sand rises almost perpendicularly above the road, falling away below as precipitately a thousand feet or more to the Pacific; an army of roadworkers has to keep sweeping and guarding against sandslides. Ancón is a resort town without hotels, its skyscraper apartment towers rising nakedly against the dunes behind it. It has a pretty harbor, a boardwalk, and still-water bathing. Ancón is a great archaeological site; and so is Chancay, where superb moon goddesses and elegantly painted black-on-white pots are still being dug from the sands in astonishing numbers—and sold to visitors at astonishingly low prices.

The coast road south of Lima passes by a succession of inviting beaches, some private and some public. Agua Dulce, at the foot of the cliff in the suburb of Barranco, is the biggest, safest, and most crowded; on weekends workers come here by the thousands, renting shade-pavilions for three soles, keeping the hot-dog stands and ice-cream booths busy. La Herradura, lying in the lee of the Chorrillos Peninsula, was once fashionable; today it is a little more expensive than Agua Dulce, but just as crowded. Its sunshades rent for five soles, and a swim in its murky pool costs ten—both within range of a loudspeaker with a cracked diaphragm playing the loudest music in Peru. Punta Hermosa, next in line, is smaller and prettier, sweeping around the curving shore to a point. Punta Negra, farther south, is a more exposed roadstead and the waves are much bigger; there is a walled-in basin for children, and a swimming pool (private). San Bártolo has good surfboarding but many submerged rocks; the beach is very clean: the upper middle class that patronizes this resort keeps it that way. There is diving off the concrete pier and fishing from the jetties. Pucusana, a good hour's drive from Lima, is a lower-middle-class honky-tonk: a town of considerable size on a protected bay, its outlet partially blocked by a nightclub in the form of a steel ship poking out of the cliff, its harbor full of dories and "Inca Kola" rafts. It is fun to visit.

From Pucusana the Pan American Highway wends south to the port of Pisco, famous for its grapes,[1] the inland industrial city of Ica, Nazca (*see* pp. 5–7), Arequipa, and Tacna on the Chilean border.

Turning back to Lima along the same road, one of the major pre-Columbian shrines in Peru is Pachacamac, the ruins of which rise from a bluff flanked by the ocean and the Lurín River. Only twenty miles from the capital, Pachacamac is a good place for the tourist to "warm up" before assaying the complex of sites surrounding Trujillo and Cuzco. Moreover it antedates both Chan Chan and Machu Picchu, having been the religious center of a pre-Inca feudal state. The god Pacha Camac (world creator) was worshiped here at least as early as the first centuries of the Christian era, and survived both the Chimu and Inca conquests. The emperor Pachacuti conquered the citadel from the Chimus and erected a Temple to the Sun on its top. One of the two Inca strongpoints south of Cajamarca, Pizarro dispatched his brother Hernando to capture it. Its golden treasure was reputed to be second only to Cuzco's, but by the time Hernando arrived and leveled the Sun Temple, most of the gold had already been sent to Atahualpa's ransom chamber. The chronicler of that expedition mentions the red walls. Nothing remains of them today except patches. There was no architectural sculpture, and all but a fraction of the ceramics, textiles, and jewels dug from the graves by Max Uhle, Julio Tello, and more recent excavators found their way to Lima. That fraction is tastefully housed in the small local museum. One can still observe the stains on burlap where the Spaniards tore off the gold plate; and a fine carved wooden totem pole from the pre-Incaic period which Dr. Albert Giesecke (*see* p. 159) unearthed. The condors that swooped about the head of the American explorer Ephraim Squier in the 1870's have retreated to the remote Andes, but

[1] Peru's upper-class drink, the Pisco Sour, contains two parts Pisco wine-brandy, one part lime juice, a beaten egg white, sugar, and a dash of angostura. The highland Indians drink *aguardiente*—raw rum, or *chicha*—the corn liquor of the Incas. *Chicha morada*, a sickly sweet nonalcoholic corn concoction, is favored by Protestant missionaries. The jungle Indians drink *masato*, an alcoholic food-drink made from the yucca root. Inca Kola, an evil yellow version of the best-known American export, has been called Atahualpa's revenge on the descendants of his tormentors.

the summit is still a fine place to survey the coast and contemplate vanished splendors.

Only the Inca-period "nunnery" of the Mamacuñas in a pine grove below Pachacamac's citadel has been restored. A more creative restoration has been that of Puruchuco ("Feathered Helmet" in Quechua), a compact Chancay ruin of late-Inca times. It lies at Kilometer 11, a few miles east of Lima on the Chosica-Huancayo road into the Andes. Its complete and brilliant restoration is the work of Arturo Jiménez Borja, who restored the small Huaca de Pan de Azúcar in San Isidro, and had much to do with organizing the museum at Pachacamac. The small museum here is in the same good taste, and its few choice items include textiles and feathered headgear mounted under glass. The building complex gives some idea of how a local lord of the Chancay culture actually lived. His home had to be a miniature fortress, for it was on the frontier, against which barbarian tribes from the highlands were pressing. The walls of two-and-a-half-foot-thick adobe bricks are pierced infrequently by small windows. On the inside there are square and triangular niches. Inclined planes within the walls were for the convenience of the llamas. The lord and his religious attendants rested on plate-like thrones. An impression of austerity strangely modern is conveyed. The surrounding fields of the Rímac Valley, still cultivated in maize and cotton against the hills of loose gray shale, remain as they were. Llamas and vicuñas in pens, and the black pre-Columbian hairless dogs (called *perros chinos* today) complete the ensemble. Folk dances, with authentic Quechua music and costume, are performed here on some Saturday nights for public admission.

Churches, Museums, Collections

Lima is filled with churches and monasteries of the colonial period. But restoration has completed the ruin of all but a few of those that survived pirates, earthquakes, and wars. Since almost all (and the best) of the great ecclesiastical architecture of Peru is within the Arequipa-Puno-Cuzco triangle, the visitor who must economize his time is advised to save his eyes for that gourmet's feast of Baroque pastry.

The facade of San Augustín, behind whose altar lie the remains of Santa Rosa de Lima, and the interior of San Francisco are first-rate; but the much-restored Cathedral on the Plaza de Armas is a dismal stone barn only enlivened by the mummy of Pizarro, removed from its bloody shroud in 1891. The eclectic marble Presidential Palace adjacent to the Cathedral occupies the spot where Pizarro's house originally stood. It was begun under Leguía and completed under Manuel Prado. The equestrian bronze of the Conquistador is the work of an American sculptor, Charles C. Rumsey, whose wife, the daughter of the railroad tycoon E. H. Harriman, gave it to Lima.

The really unique and magnificent chef-d'oeuvre of colonial Rococo in the capital is the Torre Tagle Palace, a few blocks from the Plaza de Armas. It now houses the Foreign Ministry. Its Moorish inner court is charming, its wooden miradores on the narrow street are the best preserved and most elegant in Lima, and its two-story portal is worthy of being the entrance for kings—the kings who never bothered to visit Spain's richest dependency.

The Torre Tagle Palace was built in the opulent viceroyalty of Manuel de Amat (*see* p. 46), as was the bullring (Plaza de Acho), the home of the Viceroy's celebrated mistress (the site is now occupied by a brewery), and the Quinta de Presa. Quinta de Presa, a French-style *petit château*, is now part of a military headquarters, its dainty interior flyspecked and its garden gone to weeds.

Two of Lima's many museums, and two of its many private collections, are outstanding. The Historical Museum, presided over by the novelist José María Arguedas, and housed in a building once occupied by Bolívar, who is said to have planted the fig tree in the patio, contains portraits of all the viceroys, liberators, and more recent political chieftains. It also contains some outsize academic nineteenth-century tableaux (several reproduced in this volume) which are almost surrealistic in their sharp-focus fantasy.

The Larco Herrera Museum, a splendid collection of pre-Columbian artifacts, was put together by a millionaire hacendado of Trujillo, where it was originally housed. It is now presided over by his son, the Peruvian archaeologist Rafael Larco Hoyle, and contains the finest examples of Mochica and Chimu pottery in the world. (The official Museum of Archaeology may have more specimens than these sixty thousand pieces, but its display and identification are so deplorable that a visit to the government collection is a confusing experience.) A room devoted to the sculpture in which the Moches documented their sexual habits is as diverting for the comments of visitors as it is for confirmation of those perversions which so upset the Incas.

Visits to the great collections of Pedro de Osma (colonial *objets d'art*) and Miguel Mujica Gallo (pre-Columbian gold and jewels) must be arranged through friends of these gentlemen. Both collections, unrivaled in their respective fields, are destined to go to the state.

Don Pedro's collection is housed in the family mansion in Barranco, which survived the War of the Pacific, and the mansion is at least as interesting as the hoard of bibelots, chandeliers, gold-leaf furnishings, and ecclesiastical silver it contains. The inner court, featuring a regal little palace at the end of an avenue of royal palms, is a breathtaking spectacle under floodlights. Don Pedro's branch of the family is known as the Black Osmas, a distant ancestor having been a Negro slave. This is regarded as amusing rather than humiliating in Lima society, and in fact Don Pedro points to a portrait of the Negro saint, Martin de Porras, as "the patron saint of this house." Osma is a compulsive collector. The emphasis is more on quantity than quality, and no effort has been made to select, or to present, individual objects historically or in any relation to one another or to the rooms. Yet in its very crowding and numbers all this glittering finery—painted portraits with real necklaces and earrings, ornate jeweled frames that overpower their pictures, dozens of silver stirrups, inlaid coffers, snuffboxes, mirrors, and vulgar religious reliquaries—probably gives an accurate picture of ruling-class pretensions in the colonial epoch. The emphasis on expensive materials, writhing detail and crafted fakery grew out of the hacendados' frustration, their inability to spend the vast profits of the gold and silver mines. In Peru, the high arts of painting and sculpture never ventured beyond timid imitation of Italy. Lacking the culture or the diversified opportunities for indulgence of their opposite numbers in Europe, the moneyed class laboriously put the metals from its mines into gaudy symbols of extravagance. Sometimes a single whatnot would begin as silver, be overlayed later on with gold, and finally, as the family's wealth burgeoned, be encrusted with precious stones.

The fabulous Mujica Gallo Collection reflects similar compulsions in its master but is displayed with more sophistication. In a private deer park surrounded by a ten-foot wall in the Monterrico outskirts of the city, two buildings have been constructed, one above ground and one below. The ground-story of the former, which doubles as residence, consists of a room approximately 100 by 35 feet, 25 feet high, containing the proprietor's trophies of the hunt and his rack of forty-nine high-powered guns. Skins of lions, tigers, jaguars, and polar bears cover the inlaid floor. The walls from floor to ceiling on three sides (the fourth, which is of glass, faces the park) are studded with the heads of elephants, rhinoceroses, hippos, oryx, and impalas. A hundred antlered deer form a frieze at the top. The chairs are covered with zebra hide and the ash trays are made of the hooves of water buffalo. Effigies of the animals in crystal, china, and bronze decorate the long tables.

Marble steps lead into the underground shelter nearby, guarded (no doubt symbolically) by an antiaircraft gun. When the guards have opened the bank-vault doors, three connecting rooms are revealed, carpeted in crimson and featuring eight-foot-high glass cabinets recessed into the walls and lined with velvet. They contain such treasures in gold and precious stones as even Atahualpa never saw. No doubt the last Inca's ransom chamber contained more gold by weight, but the workmanship never approached these treasures, which are almost entirely from the Chimu graves along the north coast. Chimu craftsmanship far excelled that of the Incas. And here is every variety of it: colossal gold masks with emerald eyes, golden ear plugs, finger- and toenails of gold, golden gloves, *tumis* (ceremonial daggers), necklaces adorned with hundreds of gold spangles so light that when the bulletproof glass is tapped they wave like leaves in the wind. One cabinet contains enormous tapestries of gold leaves, perfectly preserved. Another contains a very beautiful sculptured *anda* (litter) from Chan Chan. Still another features funerary "heads" from Chancay—woven bags with eyes, ears, and noses of gold. Here, too, are the finest feathered helmets and breastplates from Paracas, golden foxes from the Vicus culture near Piura, golden goblets from the Incas' tables, gold-plated handbags from Moche: 4,765 items in all. When, in 1965, 450 small pieces were loaned to European museums, they were insured for a million dollars; but no estimate has ever been made public of the whole collection's value— or authenticity. It is known that a large proportion of the spoils uncovered at Chan Chan and Batán Grande during the presidency of Marshal Benavides found its way into this collection. And it may be surmised that nothing golden of major importance unearthed in Peru since that time has escaped the notice of the astute multimillionaire hacendado, banker, and sportsman.

There are smaller collections of distinction in Lima. The Amano Museum in Miraflores has a choice display of pre-Columbian ceramics and jewelry assembled by a Japanese businessman; it is open to the public on certain days. The private collection of Reynaldo Leiza is the only place to see the painted textiles of Chancay, an art form sometimes geometric in its patterns and sometimes surrealistic that appeals to Peru's modern artists. The only museum devoted to the crafts, textiles, and beadwork of the jungle Indians is in the offices of the Summer Institute of Linguistics (*see* pp. 171–172) in the Ministry of Education Building; the work is very fine and the exhibit is beautifully mounted. The folk arts of the Quechua- and Aymara-speaking Indians of the highlands have no museum of their own—and they should have. The private collection of Alícia Bustamente features these crafts. So does the gift shop attached to John Davis' Art Center on Ricardo Palma Square in Miraflores.

Davis' shop handles the widest variety of ceramics from Ayacucho, carved gourds from Huancayo, ponchos from Cuzco, masks and embroidered bags from Puno, and dolls from all over the highlands. Laffi's, on Avenida Mexico, specializes in "touristy" objets d'art, but does handle some folk crafts and pre-Columbian items in an upstairs room. The best collection of Nazca, Mochica, Chimu, Chancay, and Inca artifacts for sale in the capital is to be found at Salazár's on Jirón Unión.

Trujillo and the North Coast

The city of Trujillo, founded by Francisco Pizarro in 1535 and named after his birthplace, lies three quarters of the way to Ecuador up the coast from Lima. By the coastal Pan American Highway it is some 300 miles from the capital and about half as much again from Tumbes on the frontier.

Though the road connecting the two big cities is one of the best in Peru, driving to Trujillo is not recommended. Perhaps, indeed, this is as good a place as any to caution the traveler about the hazards of automotive travel in Peru. Cars of the thirties and twenties and even earlier are still in use. In fact, no car in Peru is ever junked. To see a car being cranked is a common sight. The electrical system may be gone, not to mention the springs, the radiator, and the hood; what metal survives may be as transparent as the tires, but if baling wire can hold it together (and it can, for Lima's surgeons of venerable vehicles are ingenious), it goes. Wobbly wheels and steering gears, however, are the least of the hazards. Drivers are reckless beyond belief. Christopher Isherwood, who visited Peru twenty years before cars and their drivers had reached the flash point, definitively described Avenida Arequipa as a "racetrack" connecting the center of the city with its suburbs. He also remarked on the fatalism of passengers:

> They accept homicidal speeding as a necessary condition of travel.... Bullfighting has something to do with it. Just

as the Torero is expected to work as close to the bull as possible, so the chauffeur feels in honor bound to graze the side of every passing vehicle . . . the swerve corresponds to the pass made by the bullfighter's cape over the horns of the charging animal. And like the pass, it isn't always successful.[2]

Arriving in Trujillo by air, then, the relaxed traveler will find enough to keep him occupied for several days. As befits the agricultural capital of Peru (sugar, rice, coffee, cereals, cacao, cotton, hides, and now fish meal), the homes of the local landed gentry are sumptuous, and the churches, monasteries, and clubs that serve them lack nothing in luxury and gilded decor. But inevitably, as wealth and power concentrated in the federal capital, the provincial centers declined. Modern Trujillo has that seedy look—an impression not diminished as one enters the Plaza de Armas by a symbolic fountain (made in Germany, *c.* 1910) of chilling vulgarity and a ring of barriadas which contain half of Trujillo's hundred thousand inhabitants. The two largest of these, their names connoting the indomitable optimism of the Andean migrants, are called *Porvenir* (Future) and *Esperanza* (Hope).

The University of La Libertad (also optimistically named) has been an Aprista stronghold ever since Haya de la Torre was a student here in the twenties. The Apristas control the city politically, but they have made little headway in solving its problems. Families like the Larco Herreras and the Gildemeisters, who own the vast sugar plantations surrounding the city and most of Trujillo's industry as well, buy their supplies in Lima. Rising labor costs no longer make it very profitable to produce sugar, and the Aprista unions are firmly opposed to dividing up the land, which they believe would triple the cost of production, or to converting this rich valley to nonexport crops. APRA has done a lot to improve working conditions, water supply, and sanitation in the barriadas, but its opposition to appropriations for housing and to Cooperación Popular has deadlocked any concerted effort to improve living conditions with federal support.

Very little is being done, also, to take care of Trujillo's two potential tourist attractions. The vast ruins of Chan Chan, the Chimu capital, and the so-called Pyramids of the Sun and the Moon, which formed the ceremonial center of the Moche kingdom that pre-

[2] Christopher Isherwood, *The Condor and the Cows.* New York, Random House, 1949.

ceded Chimór, give an overwhelming impression of neglect and desolation. Some of the desolation is in the nature of things, for the once well-preserved walls and reliefs of Chan Chan were turned to melted butter in the torrential downpour of March 1925; but the restoration of the molded-clay reliefs at such Chan Chan sites as Tschudi,[3] Esmeralda, and El Dragón has been too mechanical to be convincing, and where the original geometrical-symbolic ornamentation remains, little effort to protect it has been made.

As for the two pyramids of Moche, one has to look hard to see any vestige of their original shape. Galleries have been tunneled into them by gold seekers, and perhaps by archaeologists, but most of the realistic Mochica ceramics (*see* pp. 8–10) came not from here but from shallow graves all over the craggy hills that surround the village of Moche. The site of the pyramids is only five miles out of town but must be reached by a tortuous, deeply rutted lane. The peasants in the neighborhood look surprisingly like their ancestors on the portrait jugs. They are reputed to practice witchcraft, and take a variety of hallucinatory drugs.

Chiclayo, on the coast to the north of Trujillo, and Chimbote, a hundred miles to the south, are the fastest-growing industrial cities in Peru. Chiclayo, capital of the rich Lambayeque Department, is a center for much the same agricultural products as Trujillo, and its industries include chocolate, soap, hats, leather goods, beer, and lumber. Chimbote became the center of the government-owned steel, metal, and chemical industries in 1943 following the installation of a hydroelectric plant high in the gorge of the Santa River; but recently these industries have been overshadowed by fish meal. The harbor, which is larger than Rio de Janeiro's and deep enough for ocean liners, is crowded these days with fishing trawlers, rubber hoses suspended in their rigging, and the smell that pervades Chimbote day and night will be familiar to visitors who have already passed through Lima's International Airport when the wind happens to be blowing from Callao.

Piura, the next city of importance continuing north, lies sixty miles inland from Paita, its port. Piura is another rapidly growing industrial center in the richest of all the coastal river valleys. Yet the wealth from its cattle, cotton, corn, fruit, and beans is as nothing to the wealth pouring through it from the oil fields ninety miles northwest. Still, Piura is a thriving city, and its Country Club, with

---

[3] Named in honor of the nineteenth-century antiquarian, Johann von Tschudi.

elaborately tiled swimming pool and tennis courts, is a symbol of progress in the eyes of the proud burghers.

Paita, despite the inevitable fish-meal factory every Pacific port now boasts, has the charm Piura lacks. Many of the homes on its narrow crooked streets are plaited of straw, and one of them is graced with a siren from a pirate ship. All along the beach pelicans, cormorants, white *gaviotas* (sea gulls), and black, batlike gannets wheel and dive for the diminishing supply of anchovies. The surrounding fishing villages, like Yasila, are beautifully situated on beaches backed by wind-scalloped dunes. Paita's whaling factory, the last of three in Peru that did a rushing business before the Norwegian and Russian fleets were able to pursue the fleeing herds to Antarctica and "process" them aboard ship, is a sight to see with its huge winches, power saws, steam ovens, and rivers of blood. Sometimes as many as twenty blue whales are carved up in a single day; the largest run over a hundred feet in length. But whatever sport there once was in hunting whales has gone today. A cannon fires a seventy-kilo harpoon, and the grenade it carries explodes inside the great mammal.

The demand for sperm oil has diminished, but the demand for petroleum is beginning to outstrip its sources. Ninety-five percent of all of it in Peru comes from the desert fields surrounding Talara, sixty miles north of Paita on the coast. The thousands of wells operated by the International Petroleum Company (American), Lobitos (British), and Empresa Petrolera Fiscal (Peruvian Government) still supply barely enough to make Peru self-sufficient in everything but high-octane aviation fuel and quality lubricants. The little left over for export makes Peru seventh among Latin American producers. IPC's refinery at Talara, the largest in Peru, turns out 45,000 barrels a day. In view of the fact that the nearest fresh water is forty miles from Talara, the sight of flower gardens, golf courses, and even a polo field amid all this sand is startling.

The wealthy Anglo-American community that has gone to such lengths to make the desert of Talara seem like home has also pioneered in developing deep-sea fishing off Cabo Blanco. Eight miles north of the nodding pumps, on a high cliff overlooking the Pacific, is the Cabo Blanco Fishing Club. Its twenty-seven members [4] pay a

---

[4] Twenty-three Americans, one Englishman, one Brazilian, one Mexican, and one Peruvian was the 1966 count. The English resident-manager, Harry Trevor Rayner, is a lonely man who gives the impression that he'd like to see his splendid facilities more widely used.

ten-thousand-dollar life fee for the privilege of hooking into some of the biggest game fish ever caught. The world record black marlin, 14 feet 6 inches long and weighing 1,560 pounds, was taken here in 1953 by Alfred C. Glassell, Jr. The record big-eye tuna (400 pounds) was also caught at Cabo Blanco, and such celebrities as Ernest Hemingway, James Stewart, Van Heflin, Ted Williams, and Barry Goldwater all tried their hand successfully, as guests of members. But in the sixties the big fish seem to have deserted this favored spot where the Peru and the Equatorial Current meet; one theory is that the fish-meal industry has depleted the anchovies on which the big fish feed.

Tumbes, the last city on the Pan American Highway before Ecuador, is ninety miles north of Talara. The desert begins to give way to an area of substantial rainfall, and in the fertile delta of the Tumbes River tobacco and tea are cultivated. Here Pizarro landed, and on his third expedition began the fateful march to:

Cajamarca

Since late in the nineteenth century Cajamarca has been connected by road and railway with the coast midway between Trujillo and Chiclayo; but for all practical purposes the airplane provides the only way of getting to it. Until the early 1940's it was the base camp for all pack trains into the Amazon Basin, for Iquitos could then be reached only by hiking through the montaña to such riverports as Chachapoyas on a tributary of the Marañón or Yurimaguas on the Huallaga. But today Cajamarca sits proudly alone in its lush valley atop the northern Andes, as isolated and oblivious to prying eyes as when Atahualpa stopped here for the sulfur baths. The royal tub is still shown, and so is the three-way stone seat commanding the approaches from Cuzco, the montaña, and the coast, in which the last of the Incas may have been sitting when his *chasquis* (couriers) brought the first reports of strange beings riding up from Tumbes with thunder and lightning.

If ever there was a place designed by nature, history, and art for the tourist's delight, it is Cajamarca. The towering rock-throne is a fifteen minutes' climb from the Plaza de Armas. The smoking baths still smoke. On the great square itself, where the Inca's soldiery put aside their arms in good faith, is still to be seen the chamber (22 by 17 by 9) in which Atahualpa collected a king's ransom only to be strangled as a concession to Christian charity. The Cathedral, and the imposing lesser churches of San Antonio and El Belén with their remarkable sculptured facades, still stand.

The few tourists who ever come to Cajamarca, however, come in spite of what seems a concerted effort to keep them away. The churches have been restored into near-ugliness and stripped of most of their paintings and silver. The smoking baths, the perfect site for a great resort hotel, are given over to a string of dirty little two-bit tub houses. The *quarto de rescate* (ransom chamber) is generally padlocked. And the spacious square where the massacre took place, ready-made to frame a Passion Play of the Conquest that would attract visitors from all over the world,[5] is given over to hedges clipped to simulate birds and beasts, and an empty fountain.

Alexander von Humboldt, who visited the mountain city in 1802, was Cajamarca's first tourist. Coming up from Ecuador's hot lands into its rarefied ten-thousand-foot climate, he thought the town was well named.[6] He immersed himself in the Inca baths, whose temperature he found to be 156.2° F. at the source. He wandered delightedly among the mimosas and willows that then graced the valley's fertile floor.[7] He was also probably the first foreigner to be offered Atahualpa's lost treasure. But after an Indian guide had led him through underground labyrinths and finally apologized ("Our white neighbors would hate and injure us if we revealed the secret"), the great naturalist concluded that the despoiled and poverty-stricken Indians were cherishing their legends of the golden throne and garden "as consolations in present sufferings."[8]

Protected, as the hapless Inca wasn't, by that matchless cup of gray-green mountains, life in Cajamarca goes on as it has since the Conquest, the "haves" and the "have-nots" going their separate ways.

Penca, the local century plant, is all-purpose to the Indians in their broad-brimmed hats. It serves as fuel for cooking (heating, in highland Peru, is unheard of); for rope and thread (the thorns are pulled out in such a way that the fibers come free); for rafters; for roofing; and, of course, as everywhere in Latin America, for clotheslines. Water is extracted from the penca, but not liquor, as with the Aztecs and their descendants.

[5] The author, who had just seen in New York Peter Shaffer's hair-raising pageant play, *The Royal Hunt of the Sun,* suggested to President Belaúnde in 1966 that its text be used, but the President turned out to be an admirer of Pizarro.

[6] Caxa-marca means "Frost-Town" in Quechua.

[7] Australian eucalyptus trees are now being planted all over the highlands to replace the destroyed tree cover.

[8] Alexander von Humboldt, *Aspects of Nature*. London, 1850.

9

In their local communities, the Indians of Cajamarca are hard-working, close-knit, cooperation-minded, rarely heavy drinkers; but on the haciendas they are accused of being shiftless, individualistic, and hard-drinking. At one great estate in the valley whose owner spends nine months of the year in Lima, whose lineal ancestor came here with Pizarro, and whose brothers' political allegiance is prudently divided between Odría, Haya de la Torre, and Belaúnde, the following characteristic response was made when a foreman was asked whether the herd of Holsteins was milked by machines: "They're too expensive so far, but we may have to come to it. The milkmaids are already drunk, and Carnival is still two weeks away. We pay them thirty soles a day, with free milk and lodging, but if they go the way the rest of Peru is going—asking for more and more without giving anything or taking any responsibility in return—we may have to put in the machines."

So until the machines take over or the Indians revolt—both unlikely—Cajamarca will remain the sleepy, sleazy, delightful town it has always been.

The Callejón de Huaylas

Midway between Cajamarca and Lima, and running parallel to the coast for a hundred miles, lies the most beautiful valley in Peru, a wonder of the natural world that has not (yet) been defiled by man.

By some happy accident of geology, the largest of the coastal rivers flows uniquely south to north before turning abruptly west to discharge its waters into the Pacific. This is the Santa, which rises in the glacial Lake Conococha, and flows gently through the tropical floor of a valley between two rows of mountain peaks before making its dramatic turn. The valley is the Callejón (Alley) of Huaylas. The black range of mountains on the Pacific side is the Cordillera Negra. The snow-capped range only twenty miles away on the other side, and rising a mile higher than Mont Blanc and the Matterhorn, is the Cordillera Blanca. Huascarán (22,205 feet) is Peru's highest mountain and stands only fifty-nine miles from the Pacific. The rocky gorge at the Santa's bend, forming one of the world's great cataracts, is the site of the hydroelectric plant which powers Chimbote's steel mills directly below on the coast.

Avalanches permitting, it is possible to drive from Lima to Chimbote, put one's car on the train that ascends to the power station, and then drive to the provincial capital, Huarás, at the other end of the valley, whence a mountainous road cuts west and south for the return leg to Lima. The alternative (until an airstrip in the valley is completed) is to drive up the coast to Casma, south of Chimbote, where a passable road cuts directly across the Cordillera Negra to Huarás.

Among Andean towns, Huarás' only rival for picturesqueness is Cuzco. But though Cuzco has the great Inca ruins and Baroque churches, Huarás, backdropped by gleaming Huascarán, is more intimate and unspoiled. As of the winter of 1966, there wasn't a tin roof to violate the mellow homogeneity of its coral tiles. The houses are built with overhanging cornices that almost touch across the narrow streets. Their balconies are painted bone-white. The doors are turquoise-blue up one side of a street, orange or umber or green down the other—a color fantasy found only here. Even the clusters of black overhead wires contribute to the harmony. And atop many of the houses are fixed crosses decorated with volutes of string steel: one of the unsung glories of Peruvian folk art.

The little archaeological museum at Huarás is as special as everything else in the valley. It is crowded with large egg-shaped stones dug up here and here alone, their surfaces carved with human and animal figures in low relief (*see* Plate 3). The archaeologists haven't gotten around to classifying them, or even mentioning them, in their books on pre-Columbian art.

Not far from the museum is a whole district of rounded boulders that convey a grimmer message. They look very beautiful, shining whitely in the sun as one looks down from the 13,000-foot pass above Casma. They are the missiles that struck 7,000 sleeping inhabitants one terrible night in 1940, and serve as their tombstones. A less lethal but more recent avalanche at Ranrahirca down the valley has muted memories of the older disaster. There, at 6:13 P.M. the evening of January 10, 1962, three million tons of Huascarán's north peak broke loose, bounced five times in the gorge, and then, slowing down to sixty miles an hour, buried 3,500 villagers. By the time the boulders reached the Santa River at 6:20 P.M., they had traveled nine miles, dropping 13,000 feet in only seven minutes.

Were it not for the vast ossuary at Yunguay, crowned by its impressive figure of Christ in benediction, it would be hard to believe that anything but peace, harmony, and plenty had ever been known in the Callejón de Huaylas. Leaving Huarás to drive north, the first temptation for hedonists will certainly be a stop at Monterrey, where a hot-sulfur swimming pool offers complete Nirvana. Farther on, a road branches off to Lake Yanganuco, which offers the other extreme in swimming (being situated at 14,000 feet) and for non-swimmers there is some of the best trout fishing in Peru. Yunguay, and Carás, a half hour north of Yunguay, are lovely towns, and in Carás architectural fantasy has created one of its masterpieces, a balcony "supported" by a white plaster tree.

As one approaches the end of the valley, the terrain changes radically. The Santa begins to boil through the steep gorge approaching the bend at Huallanca, and the road snakes its way through *forty-one tunnels* in the solid rock. All of these tunnels are one-way, and some are very long, and none of them are lighted. And as one emerges thankfully from each, the sound and sight of the torrent raging through the chasm straight below is terrifying. The tunnels were built, at unimaginable cost in lives and money, for the railroad from Chimbote—the railroad that never got tracked beyond Huallanca. That town, with its swimming pools and gardens and tennis courts for the ever-busy engineers, and its soggy shacks for the death-defying Indian rocksmiths, is a place in which to relax and contemplate the perversities of the industrial age before reentering those tunnels on the trip back.

But the most awesome spectacle in this valley of visual delirium is still to come. Nor is it the ruins of Chavín, though these are accessible (through another tunnel) on a branch road off the highway back to Lima. Chavín (*see* pp. 4–5) was virtually destroyed by an avalanche in 1945 and has subsequently been stripped by archaeologists and treasure hunters of all but a fraction of its glorious sculpture. The unforgettable vision reveals itself near Recuay on the first leg of the twelve-hour drive to the capital. Across orange-blue Lake Conococha, from which the Santa rises, suddenly appear in isolated splendor the whole Huayhuash range of giants, their shoulders casting thunderous black shadows on the virgin snow. The puna through which the road winds is too high for trees, but rusty lichen covers the rocks, and an occasional light-blue lupine or flame-red gentian accents the silvery moss where the sheep graze and a peasant woman in gorgeous maroon or purple endlessly cards her wool in the shadow of a stone doorway. Another bend in the road—another mountain range! This time the Raura cluster toward Huancayo: cathedral piled on cathedral, spire on spire, the facades stripped of statuary as if with a razor, the gargoyles sheared off at the skyline by the cutting edge of a glacier miles long, intersected only now and then by an ominous black cone or a needle incandescent with sunlight.

It is time to descend. It is time to get back to—reality?

Huancayo by Central Railway

The railway that runs higher than any other in the world (Peru invites hyperbole) leaves Lima for Huancayo at eight in the morning. Passengers are assured that a doctor is aboard. For the first few minutes it rolls briskly through the slums of straw matting and adobe brick, hollyhocks and geraniums tucked behind walls crenellated with pop bottles.

Eight forty-five. Chosica. The tracks still hug the Rímac, but now the river is rushing between gray walls of rock. At San Bartolomé one of the two forward engines is reversed (by hand) on a turntable and attached to the rear of the train.

Nine thirty. With a diesel fore and aft, the train crosses a bridge 575 feet long and 250 feet high as it climbs 5,000 feet into a waste of mountains that support nothing but cactus. In the villages violets and carnations are cultivated. The *cholo* women sell fruit.

Ten thirty. The first switchback. The train comes to the end of the track, the forward engine is shut off as the one at the rear pulls the cars up an incline diverging in a V from the dead end. There is a margin of only three feet between the new tracks and a perpendicular drop-off of a thousand feet.

Ten thirty-five. Second switchback following a dozen tunnels. Sometimes the train is only out of tunnels a matter of seconds.

Ten forty-five. Third switchback at 9,000 feet.

Ten fifty-five. Fourth switchback.

Eleven o'clock. San Mateo at 10,000 feet. An arid arroyo but with occasional green terraces. No sign of water. The motor road now comes into view, suspended by huge flying buttresses of concrete, and beside it the river hurtles in and out of holes in the rock.

Eleven five. Fifth switchback.

Eleven twelve. Sixth switchback. At the bottom of another long spidery bridge may be seen the rusted ruin of a locomotive that collided with a derrick during the construction period. When will the *bridges* rust out, one wonders.

Eleven eighteen. Río Blanco, 11,500 feet.

Eleven thirty. Chicla, 13,200 feet. Seventh switchback. The whistle echoes in the rarefied air.

Eleven forty. Eighth switchback. The train backs up around a horseshoe bend two miles long.

Eleven fifty-five. Casapalca, 13,629 feet. Snow is now visible high above the tracks. Ninth switchback.

Twelve five. Tenth switchback. Indians in costume appear for the first time. They live in barracks with their children and pigs. In the distance looms Mt. Meiggs, named for the crooked American contractor who "financed" this railroad. Evidently he is a hero in the country that honors Pizarro and Lord Cochrane.

Twelve thirty. Ticlio, 15,611 feet. Count of switchbacks becoming hazy. Through the haze a conductor appears, blowing oxygen from a bellows into the mouths of the passengers who have passed out.

One five. Galera, 15,686 feet. "Highest Passenger Station in the World," the sign reads. Remaining passengers who have declined oxygen black out. Eleventh (?) switchback. (There are actually twenty-one). The train begins to descend and the passengers show signs of life.

One fifty-five. From the window a strange blue band appears across the mountainside, pitted with gray pockets. It turns out to be the river (or rather, another river, now flowing toward the *Atlantic*) and the "pockets" are raindrops on the glass.

Two seven. La Oroya. A drab but prosperous-seeming mining town at the confluence of two rivers, surrounded by crags of ore. Not a blade of grass or a tree from horizon to horizon; just eroded slag heaps and chimneys, both rust-colored.

Three five. Lunch is served. Rice paddies begin to be seen along the rain-swept river. There is even a faint green fuzz on the rondured hills in the distance.

Four o'clock. Neatly planted gardens begin to wink among the slag heaps here and there. The first pretty village is Parco, with *trees,* and tiled roofs, but out of reach across the river. Among the eucalyptus trees move women in shocking-pink skirts. The place names are Inca poetry: Tambo, Llocllapampa. An Arizonian landscape otherwise, with maguey, the yellow conical hearts delicately scalloped as they thrust skyward out of wickedly spined blue armor.

Six o'clock. Huancayo at last. But walk slowly. The first symptom of soroche (altitude sickness) is dizziness and a thumping pain at the back of the head. If the victim doesn't take it easy the first day or two, the lower tract will rebel. As Andean towns go, Huancayo isn't high (less than 10,000 feet) but Saturday-night arrivals will dance and drink heavily at their peril. Almost everyone does arrive in Huancayo Saturday night because Sunday is the day of the Huancayo market, one of the most famous in South America.

The town of Huancayo is not particularly attractive. It lies on the Mantaro River, which drains into the Amazon by way of the

Apurímac and the Ucayali. The market sprawls for blocks and blocks on both sides of the central plaza, sunshades covering the Indian women in their black-ribboned white panamas. (If the brims of the hats aren't turned up all the way around, the women are from nearby Jauja.) Ninety percent of what is sold is fruits, vegetables, meat, coca leaves, kitchenware, plastic ornaments, and junk. The other 10 percent is Indian folk art from the region: ponchos, blouses, hats, rugs, superbly embroidered shoulder bags, carved wooden and silver ladles, jewelry, and *matés*.

The maté shares first place with the religious figurines of Ayacucho and the ceramic horses and bulls of Pucará as the most remarkable of Peru's native crafts. In the uniqueness of the medium and the latitude permitted the artists in exercising their imaginations, it is more creative than the other two. Dried-out gourds in three basic shapes—shallow plate, smaller compact ellipse with a cut-out lid to hold sugar (*azucarero*), and long-handled squash shape (*puro* or *pote*)—are engraved with an overall pattern of figures enacting typical village activities (musicians, farmers, hunters, etc.) or grotesque legendary personages derived from a variety of sources. An ornamental geometric or floral design, running around the gourd, usually encloses the figures. The artist obtains extraordinary variety in coloration. The incised background is off-white, or scored with lines to tan. The figures retain the light brown of the gourd, or are burnished with a white-hot instrument of fire-resistant wood (*quinál*) to dark brown or black. The variation and amount of detail that is obtained by stippling or scoring a polished surface is amazing. And the skill with which the figures are foreshortened on the curved surface is reminiscent of Greek vases (*see* Plate 28).

Matés sell in the Huancayo market at prices ranging from twenty-five soles to a hundred or more. The gourds come from as far north in Peru as Piura, and sometimes a big truckload of the most desirable ones brings as much as thirty thousand soles. Most of the artisans live in the village of Cochas north of Huancayo, but some come from Huanta, where the art is said to have originated centuries ago; Huanta is far to the southeast, near Ayacucho, but matés are rarely to be found for sale in that city. Ancient matés, more intricately patterned but no more imaginative, were made by a reverse process: the background was roughed up so that when treated with a black dye it retained the color; the figures were washed off clean and then polished.

Several matés carved in the old style are to be found in the Handweaving Workshop of Francisca Mayer at Huancayo, whose specialty is embroidered table sets, the warp cotton and the weft linen. Textiles are the principal product of Huancayo.

The city has a proud history. In Inca times it was an important center on the great road connecting Quito and Cuzco; Calle Reál, the main street today, was part of that road. Three times, following the Liberation, Huancayo was Peru's capital, and here in 1854 Marshal Castilla signed the decree abolishing slavery.

Three smaller towns in the vicinity are interesting. Huancavelica, three hours by narrow-gauge railway from Huancayo or four by bus on a beautiful but perilous road, was the center of the mercury mines in colonial days. Today it is a center for Indian knitted wear, including multicolored tasseled belts. Over twelve thousand feet high, Huancavelica is cold, windswept, very poor, and full of charm. Tarma, 30 miles east of La Oroya, and Junín, north of La Oroya and not far from the big Lake Junín, are popular resorts with the Peruvians. They are equipped with tourist hotels.

Ayacucho and Holy Week

Ayacucho is the principal city on the highway between Huancayo and Cuzco and about equidistant between them. But for reasons already indicated, the traveler, unless he has plenty of time on his hands and good nerves, is advised to visit this nine-thousand-foot hill town by Faucett's regular flights. If possible, during Holy Week.

Ayacucho's fame rests in the great victory won here by Sucre over the hosts of Spain in 1824, a victory that liberated everybody but the Indians. But the city owes its primacy in folk expression and ecclesiastical architecture to a circumstance of early colonial days. The pack trains carrying the Royal Fifth from the treasure troves of Potosí and Cuzco passed through here on their way to Spain via Ica or Lima. The Franciscans and the Dominicans lingered to build churches. They had already done so, of course, in Cajamarca and Cuzco, but the early churches in these wealthier settlements were soon replaced by more imposing edifices or succumbed to earthquakes or war.

Ayacucho was soon bypassed by the heavy traffic of history. The early churches survived. San Cristóbal, erected in the fifth decade of the sixteenth century, is probably the oldest colonial building in Peru. The convent of La Merced (1540), and the churches of San Francisco (1552) and Santa Clara (1568) predate all the churches of the important Peruvian cities and are unique in their adobe-cane construction. The plateresque portal of the chapel adjoining the Compañía Church is also unique. The facade of the Compañía, and the plan and towers of the Cathedral, were influential in the great wave of Jesuit church building that swept over southern Peru in the seventeenth century. But unfortunately none of these early churches of Ayacucho are exceptionally beautiful. They have suffered from neglect during the centuries of the town's decline, and from ruinous restoration in the present century.

What did survive in Ayacucho as nowhere else was the tradition of craftsmanship, nurtured in the surrounding Indian communities by the Jesuits, and a Christo-pagan emotionalism that expresses itself to this day in the mass hypnosis attending the rites of Holy Week.

The great craftsmen come from the surrounding villages, Quinua and Huanta especially, and many of them still live there, selling their powerfully stylized pink ceramic crucifixions and catafalques (at a considerable markup) through such *depositos* in the city as Margarita Melindez'. The master craftsmen of the more familiar *retablos*, Joaquín López Antáy and Jesús Urbano Rójas, have their work-shops in town and sell directly from them at prices ranging from a hundred to fifteen hundred soles, depending on size. The retablo is a shallow wooden box with painted folding doors and a peaked roof, divided into two or three "stories." On each story is a scene from biblical lore or contemporary life: "The Birth in the Manger," "The Three Kings," "The Crucifixion,"—juxtaposed with "Cattle Thieves," "Indian Musicians," "A Prison," etc. The dozens of small figurines are sculpted from clay or papier-mâché, brilliantly painted, and then glazed.

Depending upon one's point of view toward the Church's role in Indian life, the continuous extravaganza in the streets with which Holy Week is celebrated is moving or degrading. No one would deny that it is picturesque. All through the week the tempo of processions, carrying sacred images from the churches through the streets, mounts. Ayacucho's population of twelve thousand more than doubles as the Indians pour in from the surrounding villages, mill around in a trancelike state heightened by drinking, and sleep wherever they can find room. On Friday and Sunday nights no one is sleeping. On Friday the "Body of Christ," a bloodstained wooden image more than life size, encased in a coffin and supported by twenty groaning city fathers, winds its way through the streets accompanied by hundreds of the citizenry holding lighted candles. Sad but uninspiring sound effects are provided by a constabulary band, generally flown in from Lima for the occasion. On Saturday there is a colorful cattle fair in the nearby village of Acuchimay, with much drinking and dancing in fanciful costumes. On Sunday night the celebrations reach a climax. Tears and groans turn to rejoicing and bravado, devotional candles to rockets and firecrackers. Bonfires in the surrounding hills are now matched by bonfires in the streets. Roman candles misfire and singe the packed revelers, who are too exalted or drunk to care. Blind men, cripples, and women carrying babies on their backs are lucky if they are not trampled underfoot. Transfiguring faith or brutalizing superstition? (The Vatican has tried without success to cut down the multiplicity of saints and soften the hysteria.) At 4 A.M. "Christ" emerges from the Cathedral on a resplendent tabernacle borne aloft by four hundred Indians and circles the square amid pandemonium. The drunken are dragged from the gutters. The remaining virgins succumb in the backs of parked trucks. Breakfast is served by an army of vendors. And the tourist who has watched the spectacle decorously from his reserved seat on a balcony returns to his hotel and starts packing for the return flight to Lima.

Cuzco

The name of the Inca capital signifies "The Navel." According to legend it was here that Manco Capac struck his golden staff into the soil; when it disappeared, his tribe started building. From the fertile Andean valley the armies of Pachacuti and Topa Inca Yupanqui fanned out to Ecuador and Chile after subjugating the desert kingdoms of the coast and the fierce Aymara-speaking tribes around Lake Titicaca and on the altiplano of Bolivia. When they were not conquering, the Incas built here the temples and fortresses too massive for the Spanish conquerors to destroy, and upon these the latter erected the soaring, sculptured churches which combine with them to make Cuzco today a lodestar of South American travel.

Cuzco is not only full of wonders, surprises, and delights of its own. It is the base for excursions to Machu Picchu, Ollantaytambo, and Pisac, Inca fortress-cities described in the next section of this book. It has its own cluster of lesser Inca sites, too: all accessible on a leisurely hour's drive up and over the eastern rim of the valley. These include Tambo-Machay, an early Inca residence on the road to Pisac; Puca-Pucará; and Khenko, a place of llama-sacrifice with a cave containing a throne and altar. These sites are still surrounded by herds of llamas, tended by Quechua-speaking descendants of the early worshipers.

The cyclopean fortress of Sacsahuamán, which may be inspected on the same excursion, is visible from the city. It was built less than a century before Pizarro arrived, during Pachacuti's reign, and is said to have required the labor of twenty thousand Indians for eighty years.[9] Its purpose may have been threefold: to protect the capital against raids from the fierce jungle tribes to the east, to provide a fitting symbol of Inca military might, and to keep the lower classes busy during the off-harvest months. The Spaniards had little difficulty outflanking this prototype of the Maginot Line, following which ninety men with their superior weaponry took it by storm. But during subsequent Indian rebellions it provided an irksome bastion above the besieged city for the insurrectionaries. The three walls of massive limestone monoliths (some weighing up to three hundred tons) are eighteen hundred feet long and angled for crossfire. Towers, toppled by the Spaniards, afforded observation of an enemy's approach—provided he came by day. Underground passageways gave cover and mobility to the garrison. Reservoirs and storage depots took care of their sustenance during siege. Sacsahuamán's eccentrically angled blocks were mined with stone axes, shaped at the quarry, and then dragged to the site of the fortress on rollers manipulated by grass ropes. Their perfect fitting without the use of mortar was a secret that died with the Empire.

The Inca stonework in Cuzco itself is less awesome but more elegant. Many of the narrow streets debouching from the Plaza de Armas (center of the city in Inca times as today) consist of Spanish-style houses perched atop the fitted blocks—of which the famous Twelve-Angle Stone (*see* Plate 12) is one. The remains of the Temple of the Sun, originally cased in gold plates, form the base of the present Santo Domingo Church. The adjoining Temple of the Moon and Stars and the so-called Convent of Virgins are still to be excavated. The granite ashlars throughout this complex of buildings are uniform in size and highly polished.

The Cathedral stands on the Plaza de Armas on the spot once occupied by the Temple of Viracocha, the Inca creator god. It is one of the few buildings in Cuzco that antedates the earthquake of 1650, which destroyed most of Pizarro's city. Wethey has no hesitation in calling the Cathedral "the finest church of the western hemisphere." [10] The famous Spanish architect, Francisco Beccara, contributed to its design, but the work, which began in 1560, was not

[9] Victor W. von Hagen, *"Sacsahuamán, Pisac, Ollantaytambo." Peruvian Times*, 1958.

[10] Harold E. Wethey, *Colonial Architecture and Sculpture in Peru.* Cambridge, Massachusetts, Harvard University Press, 1949.

completed until 1657. The rectangular plan follows that of Seville Cathedral, which in turn took its shape from an earlier Moorish mosque. The colossal proportions and bare-walled austerity represent, Wethey writes, "the very last phase of the Spanish Renaissance ... classicism made famous by the great architect, Juan de Herrera, who succeeded as director of the building of the Escorial in 1576." Overpainting of the vaulted brickwork, the hanging of enormous conventional paintings (now in the last stages of decay), and the placement of unnecessary partitions and curtains today rob the interior of much of its majesty. The broad, handsome Baroque facade is a mid-seventeenth-century addition.

La Compañía, the equally impressive church standing on the square to the right of the Cathedral, was begun soon after the Jesuits arrived in Cuzco in 1571 (the jealous canons of the Cathedral tried to block its rivaling proximity by law!). It was completed in 1668, fifteen years after the adjoining Chapel of Loreto. Like the Cathedral's, the Compañía's Baroque interior is covered with "reactionary" late-Gothic ribbed vaults; but the splendid interior has one advantage in having escaped restorers, and its exterior facade with dome and superbly balanced towers is more harmonious and imposing. The Jesuit convent next door now houses the University of Cuzco.

The city boasts many other impressive churches—Santo Domingo, San Francisco, La Merced, San Pedro, Santa Clara, Santa Ana, La Recoleta, and others—but space permits only citation of the cloisters of Santo Domingo and La Merced. The former, as already noted, was built upon the foundations of the Inca religous complex; its two galleries contain notable paintings of the School of Cuzco. The cloisters of La Merced, containing a still greater wealth of Cuzqueño painting, are unequaled in Latin America. Wethey describes the main cloister thus:

> [It is] a work of great originality and surpassing beauty, built of the warm brown stone of the Incas, cut in blocks which are pronouncedly rusticated. The unknown architect showed genius in the use of materials and textures, contrasting the virile strength of the rusticated walls with the opulent decoration of the free-standing columns.... Hispanic colonial architecture knows nothing more beautiful than the cloister of the Merced. Magnificent handling of open space, lightness and grace combined with sturdy virility of mass, the deep beauty of the color, extraordinary richness and originality in treatment of textures, unerring taste in scale

and proportions, all this and much more make the Mercedar-
ian cloister unique.

The cloisters were partially shaken down during an earthquake in
1950 and restored by order of President Odría in 1956.

Wood carving of various degrees of competence graces most of
the principal churches of Cuzco, but no one will want to miss the
famous pulpit in the church of San Blas. This is the work of an
unknown sculptor of the seventeenth century—despite its attribution
to Juan Tomás, whose "skull" is pointed out to credulous tourists
among the figures on the domical canopy. Wethey describes the
pulpit as marking "the climax of the *cuzqueño* school" and "a major
manifestation of the high baroque at its fantastic best," but for those
who prefer plainer fare in sculpture, this busy woodwork with its
spiral columns, grinning masks, and multitudes of cherubs and
eucharistic grapes is hard to take.

The shops of Cuzco have a rich variety of native crafts and
clothing not found in Lima. Freddy Alarco's Manufacturas de Arte
Popular, which is at 567 Pavitos, is a beehive of weavers, tanners, and
jewelers working at benches under a long shed that adjoins the
showroom. Here are made stylish necklaces of beans and wood,
knitted and fur caps in the native style, and the usual array of llama
"picture" rugs and white alpaca berets. But the ponchos, woven of
alpaca wool and died in the most subtle colors imaginable, with wide
horizontal bands of intricate design, are the finest women's garment
made in Peru. They are cheap at the high prices (500 to 1,500 soles)
Alarco asks and gets for them. And so are the even higher-priced
antique wooden scepters banded with engraved silver which are
still carried as symbols of authority by the alcaldes (mayors) of the
nearby Indian communities.

A smaller shop with more carefully selected and exquisite Indian
textiles is Mayali Flury's "Nustta" next to the Tourist Hotel. Señora
Flury specializes in knitted bags and belts (*chumpis*), embroidered
manteras from San Pablo Tinta, paintings on wood, silver stirrups,
snuffboxes, purses, and very old ponchos priced as high as ten
thousand soles.

Cuzco's Archaeological Museum is much smaller than Lima's, but
its treasures are selected and displayed with more discrimination.
Two of its exhibits are outstanding. There is no better collection of
wooden Inca ceremonial vases, the figures painted in Chinese red
and yellow against black. And the pre-Inca embroidered tapestries
from the Paracas Peninsula culture are at least as fine as any in

existence, and in pristine condition. The rows of weeping anthropomorphic gods on these mortuary mantles, with the image reversed in every other row, are in golds, greens, silvers, and pinks against deep blue. This is an art form never surpassed in its perfection, even by the medieval Flemish tapestry weavers.

Machu Picchu, Ollantaytambo, Pisac

The diesel-powered single-car observation train leaves the Cuzco railway station for Machu Picchu early in the morning. It is a three-hour journey one way. The price of a round trip, including lunch, is 450 soles, and the train arrives back in Cuzco in time for dinner. But for those who wish to stay over and inspect the Inca fortress-city on a mountaintop more closely, there is a small hotel within easy walking distance of the ruins.

The train requires four switchbacks to clear the cup of steep hills surrounding Cuzco. Then it passes through a wide and fertile valley dotted with poplars and willows and large herds of cattle. The tracks now follow the Huarcando River through a steep gorge to its confluence with the Urubamba. The Urubamba is one of the two great rivers forming the giant Ucayali—the other, Apurímac, is even larger. (The Apurímac becomes the Ene at the point where the Mantaro joins it, and again changes its name to become the Tambo where it receives the Perené.) The Ucayali in turn is one of the two sources of the Amazon. But the Urubamba, which the train now follows, is a mighty frightening-looking river. Its color is generally brown to red. It seethes through passes of solid rock. Everything caught in its roiling flood is shaken like a rat and disappears. The banks are often perpendicular. No wonder the Spaniards had trouble pursuing the remnants of the Inca court into this fastness! But a greater wonder is that the last Inca soldiery permitted the single suspension bridge crossing this chasm to be captured intact. Manco Inca was killed and Tupac Amaru I was captured, but Toledo's troops never got as far as Machu Picchu; and neither did any other white man—until 1911.

The railroad continues as far as Huadquiña in the montaña, from which a dirt road staggers on to Quillabamba, but tourists alight at a small station in the jungle and transfer to a bus which crosses the river on a concrete suspension bridge and then hairpins up the steep opposite bank to the ruins. From the river, lying at 6,000 feet, the ascent is 2,000 feet to Machu Picchu (Cuzco, at 11,000 feet, is 3,000 feet higher, though it doesn't seem so). The ruins may be seen from the station, lying along a saddle of the ridge. Covered with jungle growth they would have been invisible to their discoverers.

Machu Picchu was discovered by Hiram Bingham, a historian-explorer from Yale University, on July 24, 1911. On an earlier reconnaissance of the unmapped gorges between the Apurímac and the Urubamba, Bingham had come upon many small Inca ruins. His objective had been to find "Vitcos" and "Vilcapampa," the hide-aways of Manco Inca and Tupac Amaru I mentioned by the six-teenth-century chroniclers. (It will be recalled that Manco was murdered in this area by Spanish refugees whom he had befriended, and that thirty-five years later Tupac Amaru I had been captured here by the Viceroy's soldiers after failing to cut the key bridge.) Like Giles Healey, the photographer who discovered in 1946 the great Maya frescoes at Bonampak in Mexico, Bingham was not an archaeologist but an explorer with a sense of mission—a circumstance that quickly embroiled both men in academic controversy.

Bingham was also a great organizer, and he had American friends in high places willing to back him. He returned to Peru in 1911 at the head of a team qualified and equipped to "climb the highest mountain in America, collect a lot of geological and biological data and above all try to find the last capital of the Incas." [11] In Cuzco that June, Bingham talked to Albert Giesecke, an American educa-tor who had just been appointed Rector of the strike-torn university by President Leguía. Giesecke told Bingham to look for his lost city between the twin peaks (*picchus*) of "Machu" (male) and "Huayna" (female) where local Indian *campesinos* were then working for an absentee landlord, tilling Inca terraces high above the Urubamba.[12] Bingham's expedition explored the Vilcabamba Valley, previously mapped only by the great Peruvian cartographer Antonio Raimondi, and on August 9 they located the ruins of Vitcos, quite possibly the

[11] The whole story is told in *Lost City of the Incas* (New York, Duell, Sloan & Pearce, 1948), the last of several published accounts by Machu Picchu's dis-coverer. The "highest mountain in America," however, is not Coropuna (which Bingham did climb), but Aconcagua, 22,834 feet, in the Argentine. The south peak of Huascarán is also higher than any of the peaks in the Urubamba region by almost two thousand feet. See Hans Kinzl and Erwin Schneider, *Cordillera Blanca*. Innsbruck, Austria, 1950.

[12] The author received this version of the story from Giesecke in Lima in February of 1966. The old man was quite unembittered to have received no mention in Bingham's accounts of the discovery, and indeed remained friends with Senator Bingham until the latter's death in 1956. When Giesecke gave the crucial tip to the explorer in June of 1911, the latter had replied: "Very interesting, but it's not what I am looking for." It might be added that as late as 1925, when Col. P. H. Fawcett disappeared at the headwaters of the Xingu, adventurous men continued to look for the Inca's fabled "lost city."

hideaway in which Manco Inca played the fatal game of chess with his Spanish guests. But two weeks earlier Bingham had already had his first glimpse of the famous ruin. Here is the way he tells it:

> When asked just where the ruins were, he [the innkeeper] pointed straight up to the top of the mountain. No one supposed that they would be particularly interesting. And no one cared to go with me. The Naturalist said there were "more butterflies near the river"! . . . The Surgeon said he had to wash his clothes. . . . Arteaga said the region was the favorite haunt of "vipers.". . . A good part of the distance we went on all fours, sometimes holding on by our fingernails. . . . Two thousand feet above the river several good-natured Indians, pleasantly surprised at our unexpected arrival, welcomed us with dripping gourds full of cool, delicious water. . . . They said that they had found plenty of terraces here on which to grow their crops. . . . They said there were two paths to the outside world. Of one we had already had a taste; the other was "even more difficult," a perilous path down the face of a rocky precipice on the other side of the ridge. . . . Hardly had we left the hut and rounded the promontory than we were confronted with an unexpected sight, a great flight of beautifully constructed terraces, perhaps a hundred of them, each hundreds of feet long and ten feet high. . . . Suddenly I found myself confronted with the walls of ruined houses built of the finest quality of Inca stone work . . . [and] a semicircular building whose outer wall, gently sloping and slightly curved, bore a striking resemblance to the famous Temple of the Sun in Cuzco. . . . On account of the beauty of the white granite this structure surpassed in attractiveness the best Inca walls in Cuzco which had caused visitors to marvel for four centuries. It seemed like an unbelievable dream.

Still finer buildings of coursed ashlars revealed themselves to the astonished American, and soon he was taking pictures of a temple with three great windows looking out over the canyon to the rising sun, and of the only undamaged Intihuatana (Hitching Place of the Sun) in all Peru.

In 1912 Bingham returned to Machu Picchu with a much larger expedition, bridged the Urubamba, chopped down the hardwood forest strangling the ruins, mapped the whole area, climbed Huayna

Picchu (then as now a hair-raising experience), and conducted the extensive exploration of graves which revealed that most of those who occupied the site last had been women—presumably the Chosen Women of the Inca who escaped the Pizarros. Bingham remained convinced that the abandoned citadel was the "lost" retreat of Manco Inca, and he went on to make a case for its being as well the legendary Tampu Tocco where, according to one chronicler, the first Inca "ordered work to be executed at the place of his birth, consisting of a masonry wall with three windows..." Archaeologists remain skeptical of both claims, but no one denies that Hiram Bingham discovered the most beautiful and well-preserved pre-Columbian ruin in South America.

Architecturally, Machu Picchu is a masterpiece, and its site, among the snowy peaks and virgin jungles of the Urubamba's horseshoe bend, is incomparable. But it is disappointing in one respect. Neither Bingham nor any subsequent digger ever discovered here a single piece of sculpture, or even a ceramic of any consequence. The unadorned piles of perfectly fitted masonry are a little cold, as military engineering is apt to be. And the sheer drop of two thousand feet from many of the structures to the raging river gives the visitor both a sense of vertigo and gloomy thoughts about the cost in human life that must have been expended in the fortress' building, and even its maintenance. Machu Picchu is a place no one will want to miss, but to which few will feel compelled to return.

Ollantaytambo, an Inca fortress closer to Cuzco on the Urubamba, and Pisac, north of the city and far more extensive than either, are warmer ruins in which to contemplate Inca grandeur. For one thing, they are both inhabited, and the Indians in their rich garb add notes of exotic color as well as life to the cyclopean stones. Ollantaytambo is a modern village built around the Inca settlement. It is forty-three miles from Cuzco, where the Urubamba is 8,960 feet above sea level and comparatively slow moving. Three hundred feet above the valley floor is the citadel, with six megalithic stones which were intended to form the fort's Sun Temple. Below the acropolis is a semicircle of stone steps that now supply seats for a little bullring.[13] The visitor who sees a *corrida* in this setting, with the ruined houses of the Chosen Women to one side, will be lucky. But every visitor can wander through the village, where a knot of red geraniums on

[13] For those to whom bullfighting is tame, the ring at Sicuani, not far from here, offers sterner stuff. Every May 15 an ancient Spanish rite is celebrated in which a condor is tied to the back of a bull, their struggle ending in the death of one or the other or both.

10

a pole in the window signifies that chicha is for sale, and feel close
to a way of life that hasn't changed much over the centuries.

The only Sunday market in Peru rivaling Huancayo's, and taking
place in a setting far more memorable, is Pisac's. Pisac is twelve
miles from Cuzco by automobile, and the broad valley in which it
is situated contains the outstanding andenes in Peru. These steplike
Inca terraces are of two types. Those behind the town, forming a
stairway to the enormous sprawling *pucará* (fortress), are like the
ones at Machu Picchu: steep and ten feet high. The other type is
more remarkable. A series of andenes follows the contours of the
foothills like waves the entire distance of the valley. Each of these
low undulating terraces has a very large cultivated area behind it.
The combined effect of these two types of terrace, one pale green
and the other deeply shadowed, give a background to the ancient
settlement on the river no other city in the world can boast. And
the plaza in which the market is held is beautiful in itself: gleaming
white buildings with wooden balconies, two big shade trees on which
to hang red ponchos, women in multicolored platelike hats (those
available for marriage have pink sweet-pea blossoms nesting in
theirs), alcaldes regally robed in their knee-length black pants and
scarlet doublets, carrying proudly their silver-hilted staffs of office.
Everything is sold here, from food and drinks to jackets of rickrack
and pre-Columbian painted vases. But beware—the market women,
though prepared to bargain, know the value of everything they are
selling.

The acropolis of Pisac is a thousand feet above the town. The way
leads through a massive solar observatory, its gnomon an outcrop-
ping of granite. The inner defenses of the great complex of forts
that continues to the top of the mountain can only be approached
by a rock tunnel sixty feet long. No one could possibly explore the
whole complex in less than a week. And no one has ever determined
exactly why the Incas built their biggest outpost at this precise spot.
Von Hagen theorizes thus:

> The Incas are singularly silent on Pisac. It is not mentioned
> by the Chroniclers and we have only the vaguest idea who
> built it. We do know this much. It was constructed some
> time before 1450 when the Incas tried to prevent the in-
> cursion of tribes from the jungles below the fortified town
> of Paucartambo from moving on to Cuzco. After Topa
> Inca became lord of the realm in 1473, his first expedition
> was through the Pisac gate into the forests of the upper

Madre de Dios, through Paucartambo and down into the hot lands of Peru, the home of the fierce Wachipeiri and Masco tribes. The Inca's highland army, being unused to the jungles, was severely defeated, and when the news of this leaked out some of his conquered territory revolted and he had to hurry back out of the jungles. That is the only thing we know of the region until that redoubtable knucklehead, Pedro de Candia, one of the thirteen men of the Isle of Gallo, went through this *Amuru-Punku* leading his expedition into the *yungas* of the Madre de Dios to look for his own El Dorado.[14]

Puno and Lake Titicaca

Lake Titicaca, 138 miles long, an average of 37 miles wide, *c.* 700 feet deep, and *over two miles above sea level*, is the world's highest navigable body of water. The southeastern part of the lake, behind which may be seen the snow-capped peaks of the Cordillera Real, is in Bolivia; here, two hours' drive from La Paz, are to be found the ruins of imperial Tiahuanaco (*see* pp. 7–8), the enduring religious ceremonial center of Copacabana on the peninsula of the same name, and the Isla del Sol. The latter, one of many islands containing Inca ruins, is the legendary spot where Manco Capac and his sister-bride Mama Occlo were created by the Sun. The elevated lacustrine basin in which the lake is situated once drained eastward but now has no surface outlet; the lake itself receives the water of several short streams, and discharges through the Desaguadero, a sluggish river flowing south for 184 miles to Lake Poopó in Bolivia. To supplement the plentiful supply of small native *suchi*, the Peruvian Government has stocked the lake with trout, and rainbow trout running over thirty pounds have been caught. There is duck hunting around the islands.

In 1862 the two hundred-ton steamer *Yaravi* was built in Scotland, navigated around Cape Horn to the Pacific port of Mollendo, and then dismantled and carried by muleback across the Andes to Puno. Reassembled there by Indians under the direction of a dour Scottish engineer who knew no Spanish or Aymara, the *Yaravi* still sails the lake in the company of five other Peruvian steamships, the largest of which displaces two thousand tons.[15] Unfortunately the schedule

[14] Von Hagen, *op. cit.*
[15] William Weber Johnson, *The Andean Republics.* Morristown, New Jersey. Silver Burdett Company, 1965.

of steamers plying the ten-hour run between Puno and Guaqui, the lake port for La Paz, is set up in such a way that most of the scenic trip takes place after dark. The only other feasible way to see any part of Lake Titicaca from Peru is to fly or take the train to Puno and then travel by bus or rented car along the southern shore. In Puno one may hire a launch and visit the encampments of the Uros on their islands of reeds in the shallow water.

The Uros (Urus) are a diminishing tribe of Aymara Indians who escaped the conquistadores by building these artificial islands out of the reeds (totoras) that grow in the shallows of the lake and screen their hideaways. Out of the totoras the Uros (and all other lakeside Indians) build their exquisitely shaped balsas, a curving skiff with a high prow and square sails that is discarded as soon as it becomes waterlogged. The Uro settlements of conical reed-huts are more picturesque than healthful. In fact, in 1966, the impoverished tribesmen who live off fish (and the roots of the ubiquitous totora) were being "saved," physically as well as spiritually, by an enterprising Seventh-Day Adventist missionary who had built a clinic and a school for them, floating it out to the spongy islands on a raft of inflated oil drums.

Puno, the region's capital and principal port, has none of the architectural charm to be found farther south along the lake, but it is preeminent in Peru for its dances. In December and February the city of fourteen thousand plays host to a considerable proportion of the densest Indian population in Peru. The Department of Puno contains 800,000 Quechua-speaking Indians, 600,000 Aymaras (the country's principal concentration of those who speak that language) and no more than 80,000 Spanish-speakers. (Some of the Quechuas and Aymaras, of course, speak Spanish as a second language.) The susceptibility of these Indian masses to fiestas is not merely a matter of tradition; it is a phenomenon attributable at least in part to a compulsion to escape from bitter reality. Every five years or so frost, drought, or flood ruins the entire crop on the north side of the lake. The fields of potatoes and quinoa on the south side suffer from frostbite chronically. And these two crops form the bulk of the diet of the land-poor Indians.

The fiesta of the first week of December begins with a reenactment of the birth of Manco Capac and Mama Occlo out in the lake. The fleet of balsas bearing the legendary monarchs approaches Puno, and the celebrations end a week later with dances in the stadium. But this is as nothing to the fiesta of the Virgin of Candalaria, Puno's patron saint, which takes place the first week of February.

The Diablada (Devil Mask Dance) begins in the stadium, moves into town, and touches off a series of dances, drinking parties, and orgies that continue for the duration of the riotous month.

Since a good devil mask—a fantastic concoction of horns, papier-mâché lizards, and mirror-teeth—costs at least eight hundred soles, and the doublet that goes with it, thickly encrusted with "pearls" and other finery, another fifteen hundred soles, it can be readily appreciated that most Indians rent what they wear, and that the factories and salons that supply this gear (*see* Plate 39) constitute a major industry.

Along the highway on either side of Puno are places of great interest. Pucará, not far from the northern extremity of the lake, is on the railway and motor road connecting Puno and Cuzco. Since the day-long train ride between the two cities affords a relaxed way of seeing some of the most enchanting hacienda- and mountain-landscape in Peru, it is recommended; but a disadvantage is that the train stops less than ten minutes in Pucará—little time to make a selection of the array of ceramic bulls and horses on the platform, and to bargain for them. These foot-high figurines, some glazed and some painted, are world-famous—and with good reason. The superior pieces rarely get to the gift shops in Cuzco and Lima, and when they do they bring double or triple the original price.

The motor road south along the lake to the Bolivian border passes through Chucuito, Acora, Llave, Juli, Pomata, and Zepito, villages of gnawing poverty that contain some of the most sumptuously decorated churches in Christendom. They've been moldering into decay ever since the Jesuits were expelled from Peru in 1767, but, by some miracle of oversight or squeamishness on the part of vandals in the centuries that followed, many of the gold-laden interiors are intact. The earliest of the churches, including San Juan at Juli and San Miguel at Pomata, were constructed by the Dominicans in 1590. But it was when Viceroy Toledo handed over to the Jesuits this whole region from Cuzco to La Paz and they made it their private garden that the great wave of church building began, and with it the mestizo stone carving and gold carving that covered the churches.

Juli, with its cluster of five lordly churches, is presently a preserve of the Maryknoll Fathers. With help and advice from the Peruvian Government, Father Anthony Macri (a native of Rutherford, New Jersey) was struggling in 1966 to rebuild and preserve the town's tottering treasures.

Most spectacular of the five is San Juan, begun by the Dominicans in 1590 as a structure of brick and adobe in the Ayacucho style, and turned into richly carved brownstone by the Jesuits around 1700. It has the finest and best-preserved gold-leaf interior in the hemisphere. To walk into its superb transept, illuminated by dramatic shafts of sunlight, is an experience comparable to the first glimpse of the stained-glass paradise of Chartres. The polychrome statuary, the gold-leaf altar, and the carved and gilded frames that complete this scintallating extravaganza are rivaled by the soberer adornment of stone sculpture on the free-standing columns and portals.

The Cathedral (San Pedro Mártir) was similarly rebuilt by the Jesuits around 1700. In 1966 it was undergoing major surgery that threatened to replace its impressive tower of soft pink stone with hard gray granite and its once mysteriously shadowed dome and barrel-vaulted nave with harsh brick and cheap window glass.

Santa Cruz, the oldest of the churches, has so far escaped restoration. Its roofless grass-floored nave is a romantic ruin with much the same aura as the sky-ceilinged Norman Abbey of Jumièges in Brittany. The sculptural decoration of the triumphal arch and doorways is mestizo art at its most exuberant: monkeys clutching papayas and bunches of grapes; pomegranates sliced to reveal their seeds; bananas and exotic birds.

The late-Renaissance church of the Asunción is presently a charnel-house of sculptures, frames, gold-leaf altars and half-ruined canvases salvaged from all over Juli and being inventoried for eventual replacement by the indefatigable Maryknolls. The free-standing tower of brown ashlars, though partly shattered by a thunderbolt, is perfect of its kind.

The church of Santiago at Pomata, a few miles south of Juli on the road to La Paz, should be seen last. Wethey calls it "the masterpiece of the mestizo style in South America." The Jesuits built it of rose-colored stone in the first quarter of the eighteenth century. Its facade, portals, *mudejar* dome, and rich incrustations of sculpture within and without are incomparable. "It is rivalled in detail by San Juan and Santa Cruz at Juli," Wethey concludes his properly extravagant description of this church, "but neither of the latter possesses the same unity and completeness, nor the same beauty of material. . . . This monument at Pomata would alone suffice to prove the original genius of colonial builders, and the peculiar qualities of imagination which the crossbreeding of European and native cultures produced." [16]

[16] Wethey, *op. cit.*

Arequipa and Tacna

For those who miss Juli and Pomata, Arequipa has glories enough of its own in gemlike churches and intricately foliated Baroque portals.

Peru's second city may be reached by overnight train from Puno or by direct flight from Lima, and it is a city of great beauty and salubrious climate to thousands indifferent to ecclesiastical architecture. At 7,500 feet in the rich valley of the Río Chili, Arequipa is below the "soroche belt" of the higher Andean cities. Not so cold as Mexico City, whose altitude is the same, it is comparable to Guatemala City in its uniform brisk sunniness. Comparable too is the volcanic backdrop, in Arequipa's case the symmetrical Misti, tastefully capped with just enough snow. How out of place here would be Huascarán, that dazzlingly frigid Juno hurling thunderbolts at innocent and damned alike! For Arequipa is a lady of good breeding; and if the reader, recalling all those revolutions she spawned, finds this paradoxical, let him reflect that none of them really changed anything, and that Arequipa today (unless its growing ring of barriadas strangles it) will go right on being the stylish, aristocratic, and slightly stuffy city it has always been.

It was well named. According to legend, the intercity runners of Inca times tired here and were told in Quechua *Are quepay*—Yes, rest! Until very recently the city's symbol was an eccentric American, Ana Bates, who ran a pension that catered to the celebrities of the *haut monde*—if Ana liked them. She liked Noel Coward, who left a clever little jingle of thanksgiving in the guest book, but Somerset Maugham was turned away at the door with a curt "I do not care for your plays." Naturally, in a city where flowers bloom the year round, Arequipa is famous for its gardens. And in a city whose ruling families pride themselves on their "breeding," racetracks, exclusive clubs, bridle paths, golf courses, conservatories of music, and banks are easy to find.

Which brings us back to those Jesuit churches. They are the genuine articles. Even the Cathedral, wholly a modern recreation in this city of shattering earthquakes, is magnificent. Its severe neo-Renaissance facade with widely separated twin towers framing El Misti forms one side of the largest, most elaborately planted Plaza de Armas in Peru; Moorish-colonnaded offices occupy the other three sides.

The one church that has survived the quakes intact, and the masterpiece of the mestizo style in Arequipa, is La Compañía, off the south corner of the Plaza. Its much-photographed and reproduced facade (*see* Plate 22) is conveniently dated: 1698. The earlier and less fantastic side portal has a St. James in its tympanum brandishing his sword over turbaned Moors; the sword is framed by a seashell, and the whole Baroque composition in stone is supported by two mermaids with angels' wings.

There are other noble churches and bits of churches in Arequipa, and several handsomely restored homes of the viceroyal period, but the least-visited and most completely satisfying buildings are tucked away some distance out of town on shady little squares of their own. These are the parish churches of Cayma and Yanahuara, dating from the first half of the eighteenth century. Cayma, especially, is a work of art without flaws. Like most of the churches (and even the banks) of Arequipa, it is constructed of ashlars of white volcanic stone. But here the stone seems to be whiter, the proportions of undecorated surface and carved ornament more exact. The facade with its perfectly symmetrical pierced towers and tapestried portal is like an ethereal wedding cake. The interior, with shafts of sunlight crisscrossing under the severely simple dome and barrel vaults, seems as transparently "modern" as Le Corbusier's chapel at Ronchamp, France.

One other ecclesiastical structure in Arequipa that is *sui generis* is the huge nunnery of Santa Catalina. It is the oldest building in the city, its construction dating from an edict of Francisco de Toledo in 1576. By order of the Vatican, it is now closed to all visitors. But the exterior, a massive domed fortress covering an entire city block, is an architectural curiosity as well as a symbol of man's defiance of nature.

Tacna is a symbol of defiance more comprehensible and artless. Its trauma, understandably, is the War of the Pacific. Occupied by Chile until 1929, Tacna is forty miles from Arica, the scene of Col. Francisco Bolognesi's last stand (*see* p. 70). Chile still occupies Arica. Tacna accepts neither the Peruvian defeat nor the Chilean presence in Arica, and the city is filled with symbols of its *revanchiste* spirit.

Facing the Cathedral—everything in Tacna is modern, dating at most from the great nitrate boom of the 1860–80's that preceded the War of the Pacific—stands a concrete horseshoe arch flanked by two colossal bronzes of Bolognesi and Grau in their greatcoats and walrus moustaches (*see* Plate 34). The Eternal Flame in a bronze brazier in front of them has long since expired, and there is no water in the fountain. The Tourist Hotel is another symbol: it is by far the best-equipped hotel in Peru, with a swimming pool, tennis court, and dancing pavilion, though even tourists on their way to Chile rarely stop here. Even the arid hills around Tacna bear the message: military symbols hundreds of yards square depicted in rows of cactus and stone.

The museum across the hotel and up the tree-lined Avenida Bolognesi is largely devoted to memorials of the "glorious war": a reproduction of the Colonel's sword, reproductions of the huge battle canvases in Lima, a facsimile of the telegram from Arica to the high command in Lima: "We will fight to the last cartridge. . . ." There is bitterness against the capital, too: not a single one of the originals, it is explained, was permitted to come to Tacna—"where they all belong." But along with this resentment of the powers-that-be (it extends even to Arequipa, whose newspapers are not circulated, though Tacna has no daily of its own) there is an admirable cultural pride in this city. The library and little archaeological exhibit are well run. The Casa de Cultura, directed by Haydée de Castagnola, puts on masses by Haydn and Mozart, plays by Cocteau and Tennessee Williams, and has even invited the great Chilean poet, Pablo Neruda, to come and read his poems here.

As in every Peruvian city, the growing barriadas present a formidable problem. Half of Tacna's population of a hundred thousand consists of migrants from the highlands. But Tacna is getting more than its share of federal aid—no doubt to impress the Chileans across the border—and the progressive city administration is bringing in new industries and encouraging the many mines in the region to expand operations.

The Jungle I: Pucallpa

The Amazon watershed in eastern Peru consists of the basins of three great rivers. The Madre de Dios rises in the Andes near Cuzco. Its flourishing river metropolis is Puerto Maldonado east of Cuzco and not much more than an hour's flight from that city. The Putumayo forms Peru's northern (and disputed) boundary with Colombia; it rises in the Colombian Andes. The vast jungle territory between these two rivers is watered by the Amazon's two great sources: the mighty Marañón and its major tributaries (mighty themselves, especially the Huallaga, whose river port Yurimaguas lies about the same distance east of Cajamarca as Puerto Maldonado from Cuzco); and the Ucayali which, as we have already seen, is formed by the union of the Apurímac-Ene-Tambo (with its tributaries, the Mantaro and the Perené) and the Urubamba.

The principal river port of the Ucayali is Pucallpa. Geographically speaking, Pucallpa is due east of Chimbote on the coast, and the Callejón de Huaylas. But in terms of the road that connects it (weather permitting) with Lima, it is accessible only by way of Oroya, Lake Junín, Cerro de Pasco, Huánuco, and Tingo María. In terms of tourism it is accessible by air alone. Until an adequate hotel is built in Pucallpa, visitors generally will rely on the generosity of the Summer Institute of Linguistics, the Wycliffe mission of translators of the Bible into aboriginal languages, which has a guest house attached to its base camp here.

On the assumption that the motor road to Pucallpa will some day be paved and "double-tracked" (it is now one way on alternate days in some areas), a word about the engineering feat that was its construction is in order. The idea behind this road originally was a military one. But little by little it dawned that this was a practical way of connecting the Pacific with the Atlantic. Soon, indeed, there was an arduous outlet to the latter for Peru's products: Lima to Pucallpa via the road (2 days); Pucallpa to Iquitos on the Amazon via riverboat down the Ucayali (4–5 days); and finally Iquitos to the Brazilian port of Belém two thousand miles east (4–5 more days).

The weak link in this chain was (and still is) the road. Every Peruvian President has recognized that if the montaña could be colonized it would (a) feed Peru; (b) provide fruit and other jungle products for export to Europe; and (c) relieve the population pressure building up along the Pacific Coast. President Belaúnde's Marginal Highway (*see* p. 90), if it is ever completed, will run south from Tarapoto through Tingo María to Puerto Maldonado. Since 1937 Tingo María has been a colonization center. In that year engineers, using an account of an expedition by Fray Alonso Abad in 1757, discovered a pass through the Blue Cordillera that was not visible from the air. This pass, the Boquerón Abad, with perpendicular walls six thousand feet high, was used to extend the Tingo María road to Pucallpa. Completed during World War II, the road crosses numerous trestles and bridges, the one over Aguaytía River being the longest (2,290 feet) in South America.

Tingo María, eighty-two miles from the Pacific-side city of Huánuco and a hundred from Pucallpa, remains the principal colonization center of Peru. It is surrounded by experimental jungle farms, tea plantations, and cattle ranches and could be a popular resort, for it has potentials in hunting, fishing, boating, and swimming.

Pucallpa is a rather ramshackle frontier town surrounded (perhaps in the nature of things) by eccentrics and half-civilized Indians. The eccentrics have one thing in common. They are all trying to "save" the Indians. For example:

Upriver a piece, at Tournavista, is the experimental plantation of an American millionaire manufacturer of heavy machinery, Le Tourneau, who has developed something called a Tree-Roller, which crushes and chops up small trees as it thunders through the jungle, and a Tree-Stinger, which uproots the forest giants. In this valley, which he leases from the Peruvian Government, the Baptist philanthropist is raising a herd of cattle—a herd which, when fully developed, will provide enough meat for all Peru, so he says. He could be right, for although the soil is alkaloid, he has planted it with a new grass which seems to be remarkably nourishing. But Le Tourneau's enemies, who are legion, charge that he is only creating a beef monopoly, that his employees live in unsanitary conditions, and that unless non-Catholics join his Baptist mission church, he fires them.

In Pucallpa itself is the Albert Schweitzer Hospital, founded and directed by the German physician Theodor Binder and his wife Carmen. It has been a storm center of controversy for years. There is no question at all that this region needs modern medicine and hospital facilities desperately. There is no question either that Dr. Binder has many friends among the jungle communities he serves, and that his hospital (which receives a small subvention from the government) is woefully understaffed. But like Schweitzer himself, Dr. Binder is a humanitarian with autocratic tendencies and a neocolonialist point of view. He has more enemies than Le Tourneau, they are in higher places, and they accuse him of everything from bad bookkeeping, embezzlement, and quackery to seeing Communists under every hospital bed and trying to promote the Nazi philosophy in Peru.

What both of these embattled philanthropists need is a good public-relations man empowered to prevent them from sounding off—a lesson they may yet learn from the brilliantly organized and publicized "Linguisticos" in their base camp a half hour out of Pucallpa on Lake Yarinacocha. The Linguisticos are eccentrics too, by anyone's definition but a missionary's. They win over the scattered jungle tribesmen of the Amazon Basin by airlifting them modern medicines and compassionate therapy. Then they "crack the language" (twenty-nine languages, to date) and train the most intelligent Indians to be bilingual. Finally, after eradicating the native religions, folk arts, and dress, they supply their *selva* converts with that indispensable fundamentalist stepping-stone to culture and civilization—the Bible.

In their base camp on the jungle lake, the Wycliffe missionaries lead the good life, bringing good cheer from one screened bungalow to the next on their motor scooters, eating their unappetizing vegetarian meals topped off by Nescafé and chicha morada. But the missionaries do contribute substantially to the economy and health of the region with the millions of dollars they raise for their cause in the United States; and they remain on good terms with the government in Lima by cooperating in their school program with the Ministry of Education, and by helping the Army to track down criminals and Communists with their small planes.

Whatever one may think of their way of life and their ultimate goal, it is impossible not to admire the efficiency, friendliness, and occasional heroism of these dedicated men and women. In showdowns with the mestizo patrón, traditional exploiter of the primitive tribesman, the Linguisticos side with the Indians, helping them to get a hearing in the courts when their original but undocumented claims to their lands are flouted by the greedy tradesmen who enslave them through usury. In 1956, when five of the missionaries including their pilot were cut to pieces by a band of savage Aucas, the pilot's sister, Rachel Saint, returned to the area and converted her brother's killers.[17]

Most of the Indians in Pucallpa are Shipibos. They are a peaceable people and may be visited in one of their larger settlements, the village of San Francisco, an hour's run down the lake from the base camp. The trip is made in a *pecke-pecke* (launch with outboard motor). Ages ago this lake was an arm of the river, and it is still

---

[17] She subsequently appeared on the TV program "This Is Your Life," and there were several books ghosted about her exploits and those of her converts. The best account of the Jungle Indians—and of the Summer Institute of Linguistics' program—is contained in *Farewell to Eden* by Matthew Huxley (New York, Harper & Row, 1964), with superb color photography by Cornell Capa. Though his account of the Linguisticos is sympathetic and the hero of the book is missionary-linguist Robert L. Russell, Huxley's narrative was not appreciated by the latter, perhaps because the author comments on the future of the converted tribesmen thus: "Their prospects seem dim indeed. Relegated to the bottom of society as Western man regards it, the Indian rapidly develops a desperate desire to lose his tribal identity and replace is with that of the white man. This appears the only way out of his abysmal position. However, the process almost surely assures his cultural extinction. Whether he becomes a debt-entrapped serf or a wretched day laborer, he is reduced to something less than a man, both in his own eyes and those of his society."

possible to get out to the Ucayali during high water. Mestizos have shacks along the reedy margin, and the warm waters are alive with leaping porpoises. The Shipibos still make enormous glazed pots (*telas*) with handsome geometrical abstractions painted on them—tribal motifs that appear also on their woven and painted cloth, and even on the exterior of the tiny mission church—with crosses incorporated (*see* Plate 35). Dugout canoes with a keel in the stern are still gouged out of trees by the men. The women still strap their babies' heads to boards to make the forehead slope back acutely; and they rock them to sleep in hammocks so covered with blankets that the wonder is they can breathe. The bamboo floors of the open-sided thatched huts are built well off the ground to discourage rats and snakes.

It is a poor village. The women sell tiny bead bracelets to the missionaries and tourists, but the wide headbands whose pattern imitates the markings of the constrictor have become one of many lost arts—tattooing, skin-painting and featherwork are others—that these talented Indians left behind them when they accepted "civilized" man's religion and drab clothing.

Fortunata de Maza's Bazar Chama, a little Indian shop next to the post office in Pucallpa, was displaying in 1966 a curious item from the jungle that could serve as symbol of the Indians' plight. It was a bracelet made out of a broken zipper, adorned with two rows of interlocking monkeys' teeth.

The Jungle II: Iquitos

Iquitos is the most "far-out" city in Peru, figuratively as well as literally. Overland, it is months away from Lima. By road and river-boat it is weeks away. Until "Slim" Faucett's epoch-making flight in 1922, Iquitos' contacts with Europe were much closer than its contacts with the rest of Peru. The Peruvian lifeline is still tenuous, and the Amazon port today not only retains the frumpish scars of its days of gas-lit grandeur as the rubber capital of the world, but breathes a proud air of defiant isolationism. Its products are the most exotic, its drugs are the most potent, its backlands are the least explored, its slums are the most picturesque (*see* p. 89), and its stories are the tallest. Where else but in Iquitos are love potions and dead rats sold in the same market? Where else are there scaly submarine blowers ten feet long and catfish big enough to swallow a man (they don't, of course)? And where else could the legend that the

conquistadores melted down Indians to rust-proof their armor be
converted into an up-to-date rumor that gringos were scouring the
jungle for "atomic fat"?

Iquitos is on a bluff overlooking the Amazon. It is not known
when it was first seen by other than jungle-Indian eyes. Francisco
de Orellana and his crew swept by the site on their way to the
Atlantic, after leaving Gonzalo Pizarro's party starving on the
Marañón (*see* p. 33). Iquitos was never more than a frontier settlement through colonial and early republican days. Then, suddenly,
beginning in 1882 and ending with a crash during World War I,
rubber made Iquitos and Manaus (downriver in Brazil) capitals of
one of the biggest trade booms in history. Almost overnight Iquitos
mushroomed from a village of palm-leaf shacks to a city of forty
thousand. The Gran Hotel Malecón Palace, today a shabby Army
headquarters opposite the Tourist Hotel, was one of many iron-
balconied buildings faced with multicolored Portuguese tiles. Here
came Sarah Bernhardt, and French Grand Opera. Here at expensive
restaurants guests dined on pâté de foie gras, imported hams and
butter, British ginger beer, and French champagne, to the music of
grand pianos and string quartets. And here came Roger Casement
at the behest of the British (who later hanged him, making him
the hero of Yeats's Irish Rebellion poems) to expose the Putumayo
Scandal that rocked the world.[18]

The Indians' use of the sap of the rubber tree, for balls and other
objects, was reported by the conquistadores. In the mid-eighteenth
century Charles Marie de la Condamine made a pouch out of coagu-
lated latex for his quadrant and brought back to France from his
Amazon travels specimens of the Indians' elastic sheets. But when
Charles Goodyear discovered how to vulcanize rubber in 1839 and
the invention of the automobile followed at the turn of the century,
the way for the great boom was prepared, As early as 1897 rubber
from Iquitos amounted to 9 percent of all Peru's exports. By 1907
this figure had risen to 21 percent. At the peak of the boom in
1909–10 the price of rubber had rocketed to three dollars a pound.
In 1917, the last big year, 5,500,000 pounds of rubber were pro-

[18] The story is well told, along with a wealth of other Iquitos lore of the
World War II period, by Hank and Dot Kelly in *Dancing Diplomats* (Albuquerque, New Mexico, University of New Mexico Press, 1950). The best
account of contemporary Iquitos and life among the Indians in the surrounding
jungle is contained in *Witch Doctor's Apprentice* (London, 1962) by Nicole
Maxwell, an enterprising anthropologist-explorer who sought and found many
of the tranquilizing and birth-control drugs used for centuries by the Witoto
and Jivaro tribes.

duced in Peru. In 1919, however, the warehouses at Iquitos were virtually empty. What had happened?

Although the invention of synthetic rubber was still far off, Sir Robert Wickham in 1876 had smuggled seeds of the tree out of jealously watchful Brazil. By 1896 the first great rubber plantations had been planted in Malaya and Sumatra. With the coming of World War I it was no longer economical to strip the wild trees of the Amazon jungle.

Their stripping, by jungle Indians, to supply the British-Portuguese-Peruvian rubber combine, had resulted in the shocking revelation of the British *Blue Book* of 1912. Casement was the British Consul General in Rio de Janeiro who had been sent to make a secret report on the treatment of the native rubber workers on the Putumayo River. (It was here, because of an unusually concentrated Indian population, that rubber gathering had been most intense.) Casement's report was confirmed by a document of the Sixty-second American Congress entitled *Slavery in Peru—Message from the President of the United States* [*W. H. Taft*] *transmitting report of the Secretary of State, etc., etc.* The substance of both reports was that the Peruvian Amazon Company, Ltd., had been given a concession of nineteen thousand square miles. In this area 50,000 Witotos and other tribesmen had been virtually exterminated in the wake of atrocities visited upon them by the camp bosses of Julio C. Arana & Brothers, Iquitos. In return for a few machetes, colored prints, beads, mirrors, and a certain amount of drink and (sometimes decayed) food supplied on credit, the Indians were driven from their homes and forced to bring in larger and ever larger balls of crude rubber from the diminishing supply of wild trees. When the section bosses appropriated their women and the Indians attempted to retaliate, their villages were burned to the ground. Those who failed to return with sufficient rubber were flogged, burned, mutilated, or beheaded. Those who attempted to escape were hunted down with man-eating dogs, and if they survived that, crucified upside down.

The British press professed to be horrified at these "Peruvian barbarities," but actually the Peruvian Amazon Company had been financed in large part by British capital, and there is some reason to believe that publication of the Casement Report was timed to coincide with the entry of British Asian-plantation rubber into the world market. The government in Lima attempted to curb Arana's operation in "black gold," but it proved almost impossible to determine responsibility or to make arrests in the jungle, and by the time an international commission of British, American, and Peruvian investigators reached the Putumayo, the company was already in liquidation. The East Indian plantations were supplying the world.

The infamies and quick fortunes of Iquitos are gone. But the faded glories remain—and much else besides. The city and its surroundings hypnotize one's senses from the moment the plane clears the Andes. The opening scene is well described by the Kellys:

> The most overwhelming emotion that sweeps over you is the unspeakable vastness. . . . The grasslands of Texas; the wheatfields of the Dakotas; the lakes and forests of the Canadian shield—all these in consolidation will approximate the vastness of Amazonia. Like the ocean, the horizon curls under in all directions without a rumple in the emerald carpet. . . . Like the ocean sky, the clouds march on in flat-bottomed array beyond the range of vision. Through that limitless carpet run the shiny threads of many rivers. The pattern of flow is universal and identical—twisting, looping curves as if the rivers have nowhere to go and plenty of room to wander in. Myriads of lakes—oxbow lakes, lakes shaped like cashew nuts, round lakes and lakes of irregular contour—litter the rain-forest carpet. Countless scars show through the covering of jungle, marking the former channels of rivers. The erosion of eons of geological time has worn the boundless valley down to base level so that there remains not a single speck of land which at one time has not been the bed of a roving river.

Everything about the Amazon is prodigious. Though Iquitos is only 870 air miles from Lima, the river basin will always remain roadless. Why? Because the Amazon's source in this area, the Marañón, rises thirty-two feet every year—in some years as much as sixty feet! Much of Loreto Province [19] is flooded three months out of twelve. The entire river system covers 2.7 million square miles—almost a twentieth of the total land area of the earth. In its passage to the Atlantic, the Amazon covers 2,500 miles, but it drops only 300 feet; at Iquitos it is 6,000 feet wide, at Manaus 16,000 feet, narrowing thereafter to 6,000 feet again. At its mouth, the river pours 4,250,000 cubic feet (32,000,000 gallons) of muddy water into the Atlantic *every second*.[20] It is possible to travel by boat from Iquitos

[19] This is the biggest Peruvian state and the most sparsely populated. It has a quarter of a million square miles—and one person to every ten of them.
[20] See Emil Schulthess, *The Amazon*. New York, Simon and Schuster, Inc., 1962.

to New York, and for only five hundred dollars, but the Booth Line (which began operations about 1900) has so many requests for its freighter cabins that passage must be booked a year in advance.

What goes on *under* the Amazon's brown turbulence is just as surprising. Fishing for sport is unknown in the jungle rivers. The natives use harpoons, nets, and poison only; and the use of the last two by commercial fishermen ensures that there will be few fish left in a generation. The great *paiche* (an armored lungfish with a blowhole, some specimens running up to nine feet in length) is almost extinct. The *sabalo* is to be found only in the clear head-waters. The warm-blooded porpoise has probably survived only because the Indian regards him as a sacred ancestor. Dangerous Amazonian fish include two species of stingray causing a pain so acute that some die of it; the famous piranha, a blunt-nosed, foot-long predator, schools of which have been known to reduce a mule (or a man) to a skeleton in a matter of seconds; and the even more terrible *carnero*, a diminutive slimy creature that enters the orifices of the body and must be removed by surgery.

The variety of edible fish obtainable in Iquitos—from the salmon-like four-hundred-pound *paiche* to the *piraíba* and *dourado* catfish —is still great. But the once abundant animal life has been driven so far back along the unexplored tributaries of the lesser confluents as to be almost unobtainable. The big cats and the deer, the tapirs and sloths, the crocodiles, and the herds of peccary are now far away. So are many of the monkeys, and the birds, including the toucan, the multicolored parrots, and the diminutive owl, though all of these may be obtained in the Iquitos market or from vendors along the streets. The vampire bat, and such lethal snakes as the bushmaster, the fer-de-lance, and the boa are more capable of pro-tecting themselves against man. Of the latter, the Aucas along the Ecuadorean border sing:

> Your black soft skin lies limply folded
> And shines in the sunlight.
> The skin on your back is shiny and soft,
> Not hard like the trunk of a tree.
> You just loll in the sunshine
> All limp and lazy
> And your backbone is not broad.[21]

[21] Quoted in *Tariri. My Story*, edited by Ethel Emily Wallis. New York, Harper & Row, 1965. Copyright © 1965 Wycliffe Bible Translators, Inc.

11

The fabled richness of the jungle soil is similarly beset by *ifs*, *ands*, and *buts*. It lacks minerals, and without calcium the teeth rot. Moreover it is only rich when repeating its natural cycle. One season of cultivation uses up most of the humus with its leafmold, so that a second planting is half as good, and so on. The heavy rains leach out the unprotected soil to impervious clay. The Indian, lacking fertilizers, moves to a new plot, the old one taking twenty years to renew itself. The cattle feed is mostly roughage. Bananas, yucca, and beans, the staples of the Loretan diet, do seem to grow well. Rice has been planted successfully in the river's flood plain. And of course indigenous fruit, nuts, and tubers are at home.[22]

The Iquitos market is filled with fantastic, unpronounceable, and (to an outlander) inedible foods. Sapodillas, mangoes, papayas, melons, and heart-of-palm are among the few recognizables. Very popular is the *guaje*, which looks like a small red hand grenade; the tasteless skin under the carapace is chewed. It is one of many spiny fruits, roots, nuts, and cacti competing for space on the stalls with armadillos, snails, grubs, slugs, monkeys, piranhas, turtles, and rats; not to mention love charms, coagulant barks, coca leaves, curare poison, and the popular aphrodisiac known locally as *chuchuuasi*.

Iquitos' biggest business today is lumber, with insecticides a close second. The United States–Peruvian Astoria sawmill, six miles downriver at the mouth of the Nanay, is the biggest in South America. From here mahogany, Spanish cedar, and jute are shipped to the Atlantic by way of the Booth Line. A branch company, U.S. Plywood, uses *ceiba*, a common jungle giant not good for much else, and expects to go into production of mahogany-veneer plywoods shortly. Much of the jute, which is first water-soaked to remove the outer cover, goes to Lima via Pucallpa and the Tingo María road.

[22] Slowly but surely the problem of converting the jungle terrain to a viable agriculture will be mastered, and it is possible that by the end of the century Peru, Ecuador, Colombia, Bolivia, and Brazil will succeed in making out of "Amazonia" a breadbasket capable of feeding the continent. Earl Parker Hanson, the explorer-geographer who knows this part of the world as well as anyone, thinks so, and believes that the completion of President Belaúnde's Marginal Highway will make it inevitable. He points to the rapid development of the 75,000-acre Domingo Loera plantation near Yurimaguas, where beef cattle and rice are flourishing dramatically, and to the work of the governmental agency SIPA: "After the trees are burned, the land is planted to pangola or other suitable forage grasses, and then stocked with cattle which feed on the grasses, refertilize the land, and inhibit the emergence of second-growth jungle." (*See* "New Conquistadores in the Amazon Jungle," *Americas*, September, 1965. Washington, Pan American Union.)

Lesser Iquitos exports include hides, tropical aquarium fish, pet parrakeets and other birds, and live monkeys for scientific experiments.

The tourist agencies in Lima, however, are not advertising business opportunities; they are advertising "live jungle savages." And these are as hard to find in Iquitos as rubber barons. In 1966 the bravest attempt to fulfill expectations was being provided by Marjorie Smith and Pete Jensen (former Peace Corps members). One of their two ships, the forty-two-foot *Huitote*, complete with bath and cocktail lounge, provided an "Amazon journey" with box lunches included in the 450 soles price. The double-decker excursion ship was stopping off at the settlements of the so-called riverine peoples—mestizo fishermen of Negro-Chinese-Syrian admixture who live in thatched huts on stilts along the river bank. For less sedentary customers, a light cruiser powered with a 75 h.p. outboard was taking visitors sixty miles downstream to the nearest "live jungle savages," an enclave of Yaguas who (one suspects) were being kept in pristine condition (full-dress hunting regalia with blowguns included) for the benefit of visiting shutterbugs.

Since Yaguas are the only tribesmen the visitor to Iquitos is likely to encounter, a word about their background and customs may be of interest.

This was the tribe whose "voluptuously swelling coats" of grass and feathers led Orellana to mistake them for female warriors (*amazonas*), thus giving the great river its original misnomer. Alfred Métraux describes the Yaguas of the lower Marañón region as slash-and-burn farmers, subsisting mainly on the sweet manioc root, and whatever fish and game they could procure with their blowguns and poisoned spears.[23] In 1945 their original balsa rafts had yielded to the more "modern" dugout canoe. They were (and are) a peaceable people, waging war only in self-defense and then without the use of poisons. They preferred their stone axes to firearms, and in every other way resisted change. Tribal members were equals who refused to compete. They painted their bodies, blackened their teeth, and dressed for ceremonial occasions in skirts of coarse palm fiber. Hunting was the major integrative force, followed by such other communal activities as fishing, dancing, house building, and drinking chicha. Decimated by Western epidemics and the rubber holocaust, the close-knit intermarrying Yagua families retained such shamanistic religious rites as those that accompanied medical cures,

[23] In *Handbook of South American Indians*. Vol. III, *The Tropical Forest Tribes*. Washington, D.C., Smithsonian Institution, 1945.

weather prognostication and control, and a general defense against evil forest spirits. Their mythology was universal in the sense that it "remembered" descent from the sky, descent from an original pair who were brother-sister, and a flood that at some point almost washed out everything.

The spruced-up family at the mouth of the Yanamono had retained at least their handsome grass skirts, the canister of darts and cotton soaked in curare poison, and a flask of the blood coagulant carried by all jungle Indians. Their blowgun, the handsomest of many varieties obtainable as souvenirs in Iquitos, is six feet long, wound with bark, and has a mouthpiece shaped like an hourglass. According to Nicole Maxwell, it is made of two tapering, channeled pieces of wood cemented together and given its final "boring" with river sand on a twirled rod. A skilled Yagua (and all Yaguas are skilled in this art from childhood) can sometimes bring down a bird in flight from a hundred feet or more.

Two other Indian tribes have already been mentioned in this book. These are the Witotos to the north of Iquitos, who furnished most of the hapless slaves in the rubber drives, and the Shipibos near Pucallpa, whose pots, textiles, and beaded headbands are among the high arts of the jungle region. Then there are the Campas, who helped to enslave the Witotos, and who more recently satisfied their passion for bloodletting in the Communist-led guerrilla raids in the montaña back of Huancayo. The Campas dangle from their beaded headdresses clumps of toucan feathers enclosing a switch of black hair—one for each woman taken in combat.

The Ticunas, found where the Amazon passes into Brazil, excel in basket weaving. Their hammocks, as fine as lace and as strong as copper wire, are superior even to those of the Yaguas. The Cashinahuas, at the headwaters of the Purus River on the Brazilian border, make superb textiles. The red-and-yellow featherwork of the Aguarunas is outstanding.[24] The Amahuacas are great stylists in the art of painting and stippling the body with brilliant dyes. The Mayorunas, southeast of Iquitos on the Brazilian border, are still too hostile to the white man to be approached; and this is true of certain of the Auca and Jivaro tribes east of Iquitos as well.

The world of the jungle Indian—in contrast to that of the highland Indian, for centuries withdrawn into himself and degraded by

[24] In 1966 good specimens of most of the jungle crafts could be obtained from Marjorie Smith's shop near the Tourist Hotel and from the adjacent shop operated by Jay and Edith Louthian. The latter specialized as well in handsome jewelry made from peccary- and monkey-teeth and other jungle products.

servile contact with the white man's world—is notable for its cleanliness and honesty. Few houses have doors. "People whose houses cannot be locked up," Nicole Maxwell was told, "have to respect the property of others." It is also a man's world. The Witoto woman walks away into the bush to deliver her own baby unattended, and then returns to hover solicitously over her mate, who has taken to his hammock and stays there two or three weeks moaning as if in the throes of labor. If tribal wars were frequent in the past, it was because of a chronic shortage of women; and if infanticide was a common practice in certain tribes, it was because the supply of food was acutely scarce.

The native intelligence of most jungle Indians is high. If he has not adapted himself to the "normal" ways of Peruvian life, it has been for many good reasons. When Chief Tariri of the Shapras was presented to President Odría in 1955, the General remarked to him, "It's a pity we can't converse in Spanish," to which Tariri replied through his interpreter: "That is your fault. *You* should have sent us teachers long ago."

PERUVIAN CHRONOLOGY

Pre-Conquest

c. 850–300 B.C.	Chavín de Huantar Culture.
c. 300 B.C.–500 A.D.	"Classic" pre-Incaic cultures. Nazca, Paracas, Moche.
c. 500–1000 A.D.	Rise and Diffusion of the Tiahuanaco Culture.
c. 1000 A.D.	Kingdom of Moche assimilated by kingdom of Chimór.
c. 1200 A.D.	Manco Capac founds Inca dynasty in Cuzco.
c. 1438–71	Pachacuti Inca Yupanqui expands empire of the Incas.
c. 1471–93	Topa Inca Yupanqui extends conquests.
c. 1493–1525	Huayna Capac consolidates conquests.
c. 1526–32	Civil War between Huayna Capac's sons, Huáscar and Atahualpa.

Conquest

1531	Francisco Pizarro's third expedition from Panama lands near Tumbes.
1532–33	Pizarro captures Atahualpa at Cajamarca. Fall of the Inca Empire and execution of Atahualpa. Cuzco taken.
1535	City of Lima founded by Pizarro.
1536	First Indian revolt under Manco Inca.
1538	Almagro, defeated by Pizarros, is executed.
1541	Assassination of Francisco Pizarro in Lima.
1546	Gonzalo Pizarro, in defiance of Crown, becomes master of Peru.
1548	Pedro de la Gasca defeats and executes Gonzalo Pizarro.

Colonial Period

1550   Antonio de Mendoza becomes Viceroy.

1569–81   Viceroyalty of Francisco de Toledo. Second Indian revolt, under Tupac Amaru, suppressed.

1767   Expulsion of the Jesuit Order.

1780–83   Third Indian revolt under Tupac Amaru II.

Liberation

1821   José de San Martín takes Lima and becomes Protector.

1822   San Martín and Simón Bolívar meet in Guayaquíl; San Martín retires from Peru.

1823   Bolívar takes power in Lima.

1824   Spain defeated at Junín and Ayacucho by José Antonio de Sucre.

1825   Bolívar and Sucre retire from Peru.

Nineteenth Century

1839   Andrés Santa Cruz defeated at Yunguay; Confederation of Bolivia and Ecuador with Peru ended.

1845–67   Marshal Ramón Castilla dominates Peru; abolishes slavery.

1866   Spain's final attempt to reinstate colony defeated by Quadruple Alliance.

1871   Henry Meiggs builds Peru's first railroad at Arequipa.

1872–76   Manuel Pardo's reform administration.

1879   Outbreak of the War of the Pacific with Chile.

1881–83   Lima occupied by Chilean Army.

1884   Treaty of Ancón. Province of Tarapacá, and the cities of Arica and Tacna ceded to Chile.

Twentieth Century

1919–30   Dictatorship of Augusto Leguía.

1924   APRA movement founded by Victor Raúl Haya de la Torre.

1932   Massacre of Apristas in Trujillo by Gen. Sanchez Cerro.

1939–45   Presidency of Manuel Prado.

1948–56   Dictatorship of Gen. Manuel Odría.

1962   Election of Haya de la Torre overridden by military coup.

1963   Fernando Belaúnde Terry elected president.

BIBLIOGRAPHY

SINCE the pre-Columbian peoples of South America had no written language, we are wholly dependent for our knowledge of them on the archaeologists and the early chroniclers. Of the latter, Garcilaso de la Vega and Pedro de Cieza de León are the most famous, the most informative, and the most readable. Garcilaso, surnamed "El Inca" for the good reason that his mother was a granddaughter of the Emperor Topa Yupanqui (and to distinguish him from the Spanish Renaissance poet Garcilaso de la Vega), is the less reliable of the two, partly because he left Peru at the age of twenty-one never to return, writing his *Royal Commentaries* in Spain as an old man, and partly because he felt constrained by the circumstance of his mixed blood to present both the Incas and their conquerors better than they were. But Garcilaso had withal a remarkable memory, and his powers as poet and dramatist make his account notable literature. Cieza de León was of a more scientific and skeptical temper. He spent seventeen years in South America, arriving in Peru in 1546 with the very same La Gasca mission that destroyed the sponsors of Garcilaso's father and forced the future poet-historian to sail for Spain. Cieza took copious notes, missed little, and was the first to perceive that other great civilizations had preceded the Incas.[1]

The most thorough account of those civilizations is contained in Victor Wolfgang von Hagen's *The Desert Kingdoms of Peru* (Greenwich, Connecticut, New York Graphic Society Publishers,

---

[1] *The Incas of Pedro de Cieza de León* has been edited by Victor Wolfgang von Hagen and translated by Harriet de Onís (Norman, Oklahoma, University of Oklahoma Press, 1959). Garcilaso's work is available in an Avon paperback of 1961, translated by Maria Jolas and edited by Alain Gheerbrant.

Ltd., 1965), a book that is notable also for two essentials in which other archaeologists are almost always deficient: a felicitous style and photographs equal to bringing the past to life visually. There are many modern studies of the Incas, but the two I have found most helpful are J. Alden Mason's *The Ancient Civilizations of Peru* (Baltimore, Maryland, Penguin Books, Inc., 1957) and Louis Baudin's *A Socialist Empire: The Incas of Peru* (Princeton, New Jersey, D. Van Nostrand Company, Inc., 1961), more specialized but fascinating for its account of how the system functioned socially and economically. *Lost City of the Incas* (New York, Duell, Sloan & Pearce, 1948) and other earlier books by Machu Picchu's discoverer, Hiram Bingham of Yale University, are interesting but flawed by an obsession to prove an unprovable theory.

William Hickling Prescott's *Conquest of Mexico and Conquest of Peru* (New York, Modern Library, 1936), though written over a century ago by a proper Bostonian who never visited Peru, or even Spain, and who was virtually blind when he wrote it, has never seriously been faulted in accuracy, and for dramatic power and stylistic elegance has no superior in the whole literature of historical writings. Archaeology has made some of Prescott's account of pre-Conquest Peru inadequate, but his narrative of the Conquest itself and the civil wars that followed stands up splendidly.

For the four hundred years of Peruvian history that follow, there are no standard sources. The colonial period is virtually a blank, and perhaps deserves to be: it was an age of social and aesthetic stagnation. Only ecclesiastical architecture and its attendant arts left a rich heritage, and this special field has been exhaustively and perceptively documented by Harold E. Wethey of Harvard University in his *Colonial Architecture and Sculpture in Peru* (Cambridge, Massachusetts, Harvard University Press, 1949). The period of independence can only be glimpsed sidewise through biographies of Bolívar, San Martín, Sucre, Lord Cochrane, and other participants. Salvador de Madariaga's *Bolívar* (New York, Pellegrini & Cudahy, 1952) and Ricardo Rojas' *San Martín, Knight of the Andes;* translated by Herschel Brickell and Carlos Videla (New York, Doubleday & Company, Inc., 1945) are outstanding. The abortive revolt of Tupac Amaru II that preceded the independence is covered in *The Last Inca Revolt 1780–83* by Lillian Estelle Fisher (Norman, Oklahoma, University of Oklahoma Press, 1965). In this period, Charles Marie de la Condamine (1746) and Alexander von Humboldt (1802) were the first Peru travelers, but Condamine has never been translated, and the notebooks of the German geographer-botanist have never even been printed, though many of Humboldt's observations are scattered through other books.

The nineteenth century is revealed to us through the memoirs of a number of Victorian Age diplomats and antiquarians, of whom the American Ephraim Squier, the Englishman Sir Clements Markham, and the Swiss Johann von Tschudi have left the most interesting accounts.

The twentieth century is glimpsed less comprehensively but sometimes more sharply in such travel books as Christopher Isherwood's *The Condor and the Cows* (New York, Random House, 1949), Sacheverell Sitwell's *Golden Wall and Mirador* (Cleveland, Ohio, World Publishing Co., 1961) and *Dancing Diplomats* (Iquitos in the Forties) by Hank (Henry Warren) and Dot (D.T.S.) Kelly (Albuquerque, New Mexico, University of New Mexico Press, 1950). George Kubler's brilliant Smithsonian Institution paper of 1952, *The Indian Caste of Peru, 1795–1940. A Population Study Based upon Tax Records and Census Reports*, provides unique insights into the devious arrangements under which the Indians have always been exploited. A short but caustically realistic monograph on the country's social economy is Professor R. J. Owens' *Peru* (Oxford University Press, 1963). Victor Raúl Haya de la Torre and Fernando Belaúnde Terry have written glowingly of their visions. President Belaúnde's *Peru's Own Conquest* (Lima, 1965) has been translated into English by David A. Robinson, whose own *Peru in Four Dimensions* (Lima, 1964) provides a valuable statistical abstract of the Belaúnde reform era.

Hubert Herring's *A History of Latin America* (New York, Alfred A. Knopf, Inc., 1955) and John E. Fagg's *Latin America: A General History* (New York, Macmillan Company, 1963) are the best works in their enormous field.

The novels of Ciro Alegria, and Mario Vargas Llosa's *The Time of the Hero* (New York, Grove Press, 1966) and Sebastian Salazar Bondy's *Lima la horrible* (Mexico, D. F., Ediciones S. A., 1964) offer insights into modern Peru by Peruvian authors of unusual discernment. Two of Alegria's works have appeared in English: *Broad and Alien Is the World* (Chester Springs, Pennsylvania, Dufour Editions, 1963), and *Golden Serpent* (New York, New American Library).

INDEX

of persons mentioned in the text

Abad, Alonso, 170
Alarco, Freddy, 157
Alegria, Ciro, 63n.
Alexander, Robert J., 79n.
Almagro, Diego de, 23, 29, 31, 33
Almagro the Younger, 33, 34
Alvarado, Pedro de, 23, 30
Amat, Manuel de, 46, 52, 137
Arana, Julio C., 175
Areche, Antonio de, 47
Arguedas, José María, 137
Atahualpa, 15, 24, 25, 27, 28, 29, 30, 33, 135, 144, 145

Balboa, Vasco Núñez de, 23
Balta, José, 64, 65, 66, 67
Baquedano, Manuel, 71
Bard, H. Edwin, 78
Basadre, Jorge, 59n.
Bates, Ana, 167
Baudin, Louis, 17, 19, 39
Beccara, Francisco, 155
Belaúnde Terry, Fernando, v, 22, 67, 80, 83, 84, 85, 87–93, 145n., 146, 170, 178n.
Belaúnde, Victor Andrés, 87
Beltrán, Pedro, 87, 90
Benalcázar, Sebastián de, 37
Benavides, Oscar, 81, 82, 139
Bermúdez, Morales, 72, 73
Bernhardt, Sarah, 174
Billinghurst, Guillermo, 76
Binder, Theodor and Carmen, 171
Bingham, Alfred M., vi
Bingham, Hiram, 13n., 20n., 159–161
Bolívar, Simón, 49, 50, 51, 52–59, 61, 64, 66, 137

Bolognesi, Francisco, 70, 71, 168, 169
Borja, Arturo Jiménez, 136
Brandsen, General, 52
Bustamante, Alícia, 140
Bustamante Rivero, José, 82, 83

Cáceres, Andrés, 71, 72, 73
Calderón, García, 38, 71
Campusano, Rosa, 52
Candamo, Manuel, 73
Candia, Pedro de, 163
Carvajal, Francisco de, 36, 37
Casas, Bartolomé de Las. *See* Las Casas, Bartolomé de.
Casement, Roger, 174, 175
Castagnola, Haydée de, 169
Castilla, Ramón, 59, 61, 62, 64, 152
Charles III, 10, 39, 46, 47
Charles IV, 10
Charles V, 24, 25, 35
Cochrane, Admiral Lord, 52, 53, 70, 150
Condamine, Charles Marie de la, 174
Cieza de León, 15, 16n., 20
Cornejo Chavez, Hector, 87
Cortés, Hernando, 22
Cuauhtémoc, 22

Davis, John, v, 140
De Soto, Hernando, 24, 26, 29, 30
Diez Canseco, Pedro, 64, 65, 66, 87
Duell, Charles, vi

Echenique, José Rufino, 63

Fagg, John E., 76n.
Faucett, Elmer J., 132, 173

Fawcett, Col. P. H., 159n.
Fisher, Lillian Estelle, 48n.
Flury, Mayali, 157
Freyer, Frank B., 78

Galdames, Luis, 71n.
Gamarra, Agustín, 60, 61
Garcia, Aleixo, 15
Garcilaso de la Vega, 13, 24n., 27, 28n., 47
Garrido, José Eulógio, 81
Gasca, Pedro de la, 35, 36, 37
Giesecke, Albert, 78, 135, 159
Gildemeister (family), 141
Glassell, Alfred C., Jr.; 144
Goodyear, Charles, 174
Grace, W. R. and Michael, 72, 77
Grau, Miguel, 70, 71n., 168
Griffis, Donald, Sr., vi
Guiriór, Manuel, 47
Gutiérrez, Tomás, 66

Hagen, Victor Wolfgang von, 7, 8, 11n., 16n., 155n., 162
Hanke, Lewis, 58n.
Hanson, Earl Parker, 178n.
Haya de la Torre, Victor Raúl, v, 73, 78, 79, 80, 81, 82, 83, 87, 88, 90, 92, 141, 146
Healey, Giles, 159
Herring, Hubert, 39, 42n., 45, 57n., 59n.
Heyerdahl, Thor, 4
Hinojosa, Pedro de, 36
Holmberg, Alan, 86n.
Huáscar, 15, 16, 24, 25, 27
Huayna Capac, 15, 31
Humboldt, Alexander von, 10, 62, 145
Hutchinson, Thomas J., 67n.
Huxley, Matthew, 172n.

Iglesias, Miguel, 71
Isherwood, Christopher, 140

Jensen, Pete, 179
Johnson, William Weber, 163n.
Juan y Santacilia, Jorge, 43n.

Kelly, Hank and Dot, 174n., 176
Kennedy, John F., 87
Kinzl, Hans, 159n.
Kubler, George, 43n., 63, 85

Lamar, José de, 59, 60
Larco Herrera, Rafael, 11, 137, 140
Larco Hoyle, Rafael, 11, 137

Las Casas, Bartolomé de, 22, 34, 38, 39, 49, 58
La Serna, General, 51
Lautaro, 50
Lavalle, Hernando, 83
Le Corbusier, 9, 168
Leguia, Augusto, 73, 75, 76, 77, 83, 84, 137
Leiza, Reynaldo, 139
Le Tourneau, 171
Loayza, Francisco, 45
Loayza, Tomás, v
Loera, Domingo, 178n.
López Antáy, Joaquín, 153
Lothrop, S. K., 29
Louthian, Edith and Jay, 180n.
Ludwig, Emil, 54n., 59n.
Luque, Hernando de, 23
Lynch, Patricio, 71

Macri, Anthony, 165
Madariaga, Salvador de, 53n.
Manco Capac, 13, 154, 163, 164
Manco Inca, 30, 31–35, 47, 158, 160
Mar, Marshal del, 64
Mariátegui, Carlos, 74
Markham, Sir Clements, 41n., 60, 70n.
Martínez de Compañon, 10
Mason, J. Alden, 4n., 8, 14n., 18
Maxwell, Nicole, 174n., 180
Mayer, Francisca, 151
Maza, Fortunata de, 173
Meiggs, Henry, 64, 65, 133, 150
Melindez, Margarita, 153
Mendoza, Antonio de, 40
Metraux, Alfred, 179
Miller, William, 52
Mises, Ludwig von, 17
Montero, Lizardo, 71
Montezuma, 27
Mujica Gallo, Miguel, 10, 137, 138

Neruda, Pablo, x, 169
Núñez Vela, Blasco, 34, 35

Odría, Manuel, 75, 80, 82, 84–88, 146, 157, 181
O'Higgins, Bernardo, 51, 61
Orbegoso, Luis José, 60, 61
Orellana, Francisco de, 33, 174, 179
Orrego Villacorte, Eduardo, v
Osma, Pedro de, 137, 138
Owens, R. J., 68, 69n.

Pachacuti Inca Yupanqui, 13, 14, 155
Palma, Ricardo, 72

Pardo y Barreda, José, 73, 75, 76
Pardo, Manuel, 66, 67, 68, 69, 73, 75, 90
Paz Estenssoro, Victor, 84
Pedrarias Dávila, 23
Perricholi, La, 46, 52
Pezet, Juan Antonio, 64
Pezuela, Viceroy, 51
Philip II, 41
Piérola, Nicolás de, 67–71, 75, 76
Pizarro, Francisco, 16, 17, 22–37, 39, 67, 133, 136, 140, 144, 146, 150, 155
Pizarro, Gonzalo, 31, 32, 33–37, 174
Pizarro, Hernando, 26, 29, 31, 32, 135
Pizarro, Juan, 31
Pizarro, Pedro, 25
Prada, Manuel González, 73, 74
Prado, Manuel, 80, 81, 82, 83, 85, 86, 88, 137
Prado, Mariano Ignacio, 64, 67, 69, 70
Prat, Arturo, 71n.
Prescott, William H., 24, 25n., 27, 37
Priale, Ramiro, 83

Raimondi, Antonio, 159
Reiche, Maria, 6
Robinson, David A., v, 86n., 89n., 91n.
Rodríguez, Simón, 49
Romaña, Eduardo López de la, 73
Rojas, Ricardo, 52n., 56n.
Rumsey, Charles G., 137
Russell, Robert L., 172

Sáenz, Manuela, 50, 61
Saint, Rachel, 172
Salaverry, Felipe Santiago de, 60, 61
Sánchez Cerro, Luis, 78, 79, 81
San Martín, José de, 50, 51, 52, 53, 54, 55, 56, 57, 61
San Román, President, 64
Santa Cruz, Andrés, 59, 60, 61
Santa Rosa de Lima, 136
Schaffer, Peter, 145n.
Schneider, Erwin, 159n.

Schulthess, Emil, 176n.
Sitwell, Sacheverell, 10
Smith, Marjorie, 179, 180n.
Squier, Ephraim, 11, 135
Stewart, Watt, 66n.
Sucre, José Antonio de, 52, 53, 56, 152
Sutton, C. W., 78

Tariri, Chief, 177n., 181
Tello, Julio C., 4, 6, 7, 135
Toledo, Francisco de, 40, 41, 42, 43, 47, 158, 168
Tomás, Juan, 157
Topa Inca Yupanqui, 14, 162
Toparca, 30
Torre Tagle, Marquis of, 52, 53
Townsend, Andrés, v
Tschudi, Johann von, 142n.
Tupac Amaru I, 41, 158
Tupac Amaru II, 46, 47, 49, 58

Ugarte, Alfonso, 70
Uhle, Max, 6, 135
Ulloa, Antonio de, 43n.
Urbano Rojas, Jesús, 153

Vaca de Castro, 32, 33, 34, 35
Valdivia, Pedro de, 32, 37, 50
Vallejo, César, 81
Valverde, Vicente de, 27, 29, 30
Vasconcelos, José, 79
Vier, Luis, vi
Viracocha (Inca), 13
Viracocha (Creator), 44
Vivanco, Agostín, 61, 63

Wallis, Ethel Emily, 177n.
Weiner, Charles, 11
Wethey, Harold E., 155n., 156, 157, 166
Wickham, Robert, 175
Wilder, Thornton, 44
Willimetz, Emil, v
Wright, Frank Lloyd, 89

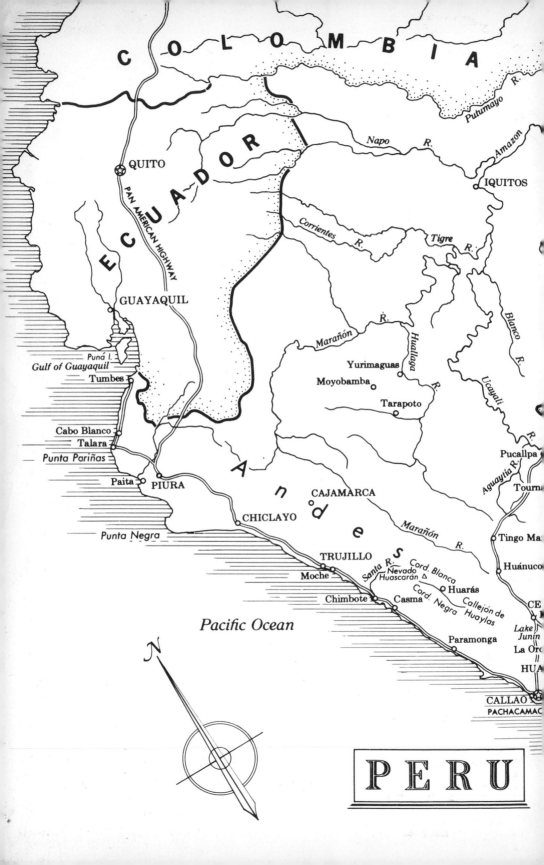